"In my life as a professional athlete and businessman, I've been privileged to know some of the greatest leaders, pastors, athletes and coaches around the world. Jeff Leake, without a doubt, ranks among the finest of all. Even in a room with thousands of people, he somehow makes you feel important. This is clearly a result of his one-on-one time with Jesus in prayer. I strongly encourage all to read this book knowing the author is as authentic as they come."

—Stephen J. Avery, former Pittsburgh Steeler, Avery Family Ministries, Pittsburgh, PA

"This prayer guide has personally equipped me to pray powerful, biblical declarations over my life, family, and ministry and has helped to greatly enhance my prayer life. As a pastor, I have used this resource when instructing and encouraging new believers to go to the next level in their individual time with God. It is simple, user-friendly, and greatly effective."

—Kate Griffin, women's pastor at Allison Park Church, Pittsburgh, PA

"Jeff Leake is a gifted communicator, and he uses his skill to lead us to another level of communication with God. Jeff's personal insight is fresh and encouraging. This devotional opens Scripture to reveal how God's message is relevant to us and how it applies to our personal challenges and daily routines. It directs us on a purposeful path to an awareness that God is for us and His Word is the bridge to a marvelous, meaningful relationship with Him."

—Patty Edwards, administrative assistant for Pareto Consulting, Evans City, PA

"Jeff's creative approach in *Praying with Confidence* is a proven, 'how to' teaching that will turn your guilt-ridden, ineffective daily prayer time into an anticipated, meaningful time with Christ. Pastors, this is a must tool for your people and for you too!"

—Ron Heitman, lead pastor, Evangel Church

"A proven tool, *Praying with Confidence* will give you the help you need to develop a consistent and passionate life of engagement with God!"

—Ron Johnson, lead pastor, One Church, Orlando, FL

"This book doesn't just talk about prayer but actually guides you to engage in prayer. It's a practical guide that includes fresh ways to pray and interact with God on a daily basis."

—Cullen Allen, executive pastor, Allison Park Church, Pittsburg, PA

D0109044

What people are saying about *Praying with Confidence* . . .

"Jeff has a great life, a great family, a great church, and he's exactly the right person to write a devotional book for your spiritual life! You will enjoy the journey as you grow spiritually!"

—Rob Ketterling, lead pastor, River Valley Church, Savage, MN

"Jeff doesn't just provide a practical devotional tool, he shares his story. The kingdom fruit produced in his life is proportional to his personal walk with the Lord. This guide will answer your questions and help you nurture your own personal relationship with Jesus!"

—John Van Pay, lead pastor, Gateway Fellowship, San Antonio, TX

"With this practical guidance and wisdom anyone can experience a deeper understanding of God. Jeff Leake demonstrates what it truly means to live a life of prayer. As a result he has heard the voice of the Lord and created innovative ways to reach lost people. Discover how to grow in *your* prayer life. I know you'll be inspired!"

—Brian Bolt, president, CityReach Network

"When I think of my friend Jeff Leake I think of a man who practices what he preaches! As soon as I heard that he had written this book I wanted to read it. I want to learn new insights on prayer from a man who actually prays. Open your heart and don't just read the words but feel the passion Jeff has for daily communion with the Father."

—Rich Wilkerson, lead pastor, Trinity Church, Miami

"I highly recommend *Praying with Confidence* as a tool to assist any believer in developing their devotional life and in learning how to pray bold prayers. My good friend Jeff Leake has demonstrated great insight into the process and pathway of effective prayer."

—Scott Wilson, coauthor of *Clear the Stage: Making Room for God;* senior pastor of the Oaks Fellowship, Red Oaks, TX

"For those seasons of life when communicating with God feels difficult or confusing, we need a helpful structure and path to guide our prayers. Pastor Jeff's book offers a clear, easy-to-follow way to connect with the One who loves us unconditionally. I'm grateful for this resource to support my journey to follow Jesus."

—Jane Abbate, author of *Where Do Broken Hearts Go?* *Healing and Hope After Abortion*

"Almost every Christian I know wants to get better at prayer. Who better to learn from then someone with a proven track record of praying consistent prayers that get results? I have had the privilege of watching Jeff Leake pray for over a decade. In addition to teaching me how to pray, his prayers have actually shifted my life in dramatic ways. His ability to connect with God, and hear from God, has led to many insights that he was able to apply directly to my life during moments of decision. If you want to learn to pray effective prayers that get God's attention, this book will be a catalyst for you."

—Brad Leach, lead pastor, CityLife Church, Philadelphia, PA

"As a pastor, it's my goal to help people connect to God's presence on a daily basis. Jeff's *Praying with Confidence* is an invaluable and practice resource I plan to use to help accomplish this goal. This easy-to-follow, scripturally based prayer guide is a catalyst of spiritual growth for churches as well as individuals. I highly recommend it for anyone wanting to grow in their prayer life."

—Russ Horne, lead pastor, Sharpsburg Family Worship Center, Sharpsburg, PA

"Jeff's prayer guide really is a daily journey—a path that leads to the presence of Jesus Himself. What I love about this prayer guide is that it presents thirty-one fresh and unique ways to interact with Scripture through prayer. Each day is different from the next and each model is powerful and effective. I recommend it to new followers of Jesus and seasoned believers alike."

—Chris Griffin, Hampton campus pastor, Allison Park Church, Allison Park, PA

"This 31-day prayer journey is more than a traditional devotional; it's a tutorial of methods to derive the most from God's Word. Pastor Jeff guides the reader into unlocking and applying God's biblical message to carry the power of the Holy Spirit to our lives and to those all around us!"

—David Gianamore, product line manager, Eaton Electronic Manufacturing, Pittsburgh, PA

"I appreciate how Jeff extracts declarative prayer points out of Scripture passages that bring power and focus to life situations. God has used this devotional to draw me closer to His presence, give me greater insight on Scripture, and increase my boldness in declaring the promises of God. This devotional is a great introduction to new believers beginning their journey of prayer, and also a powerful prayer tool to those who have been in the faith for a long time. I plan to give this devotional as a gift and encourage people who are walking through problems to commit to using this as their daily devotional for thirty-one days to see how their perspective on their problems changes. If you desire to intensify your prayer time, I highly recommend this powerful prayer tool."

—Debbie Lynch, pastoral care pastor, Allison Park Church, Allison Park, PA

"From the east African thousand hills to North Hills of Pittsburgh, Pennsylvania, Jeff Leake has helped me grow from a baby in spiritual things to becoming a mature man of God. The prayer guide he developed has helped me grow in my devotional moments from a doubtful intercessor to a prayer warrior."

—Bertin Ntampaka, student, Berean School of the Bible

PRAYING WITH CONFIDENCE

31 DAYS OF POWERFUL MOMENTS WITH GOD

JEFF LEAKE

SALUBRIS
RESOURCES

PRAYING WITH CONFIDENCE

Copyright © 2015 by Jeff Leake

ALL RIGHTS RESERVED

Published by Salubris Resources
1445 N. Boonville Ave.
Springfield, Missouri 65802

www.salubrisresources.com

No part of this book may be reproduced, stored in a retrieval system, or transmitted in any form or by any means—electronic, mechanical, photocopy, recording, or, otherwise—without prior written permission of the publisher, except for brief quotations used in connection with reviews in magazines or newspapers.

Cover design by PlainJoe Studios (www.plainjoestudios.com)
Interior design by Tom Shumaker

Produced with the assistance of Livingstone, the Publishing Services Division of Barton-Veerman Company. Project staff includes: Bruce Barton, Ashley Taylor and Tom Shumaker.

Unless otherwise specified, all Scripture quotations are taken from the Holy Bible, New International Version®, NIV®. Copyright © 1973, 1978, 1984, 2011 by Biblica, Inc.™ Used by permission of Zondervan. All rights reserved worldwide.www.zondervan.com. The "NIV" and "New International Version" are trademarks registered in the United States Patent and Trademark Office by Biblica, Inc.™

Scripture quotations marked KJV are from the King James Version, and are held in public domain.

Scripture quotations marked NKJV are from the New King James Version of the Bible®. ©1982 by Thomas Nelson, Inc. Used by permission. All rights reserved.

ISBN: 978-1-68067-039-4

Printed in the United States of America

19 18 17 16 15 • 1 2 3 4 5

CONTENTS

CHAPTER 1

AM I DOING THIS RIGHT?

Prayer is one of the most powerful, mysterious, and vulnerable practices that we ever attempt in life.

Think about it! When you pray effectively and with a raw heart:

- ✧ Needs are met
- ✧ Bodies are healed
- ✧ Finances are provided
- ✧ Peace is released
- ✧ Wisdom is granted
- ✧ Lives are changed
- ✧ Heaven is pleased

It's an awesome moment when you know that your prayers have touched God and that God has responded on your behalf. But what about all the other moments when we feel like absolutely nothing is happening? What about those moments when we pray and we wonder if God is listening? Or maybe we feel like we just don't really understand how to do this "prayer thing" like others are doing.

My First Steps in Prayer

When I was fifteen years old, I made the decision to commit my life to Christ. It was at a youth camp near Indiana, Pennsylvania, when I responded to a challenge to surrender everything to Him. That moment of decision changed me. I knew that God was doing something in my life. I felt clean. I felt renewed. I was ready to take steps toward His plan for my life.

Shortly after that encounter with God, my youth pastor told me that I needed to establish a prayer life that was more developed than the sporadic times of prayer I was used to. He told me that I should get up early enough every day to spend at least fifteen minutes in prayer.

So I tried it.

My alarm sounded and I bounced out of bed ready for my first experiment in developing a prayer life. Because I had grown up in the church, I had heard about great men and women of God who prayed for an hour a day or more. This was my ambition—to be one of those prayer warriors. I was ready to accept the steps to achieving my plan.

I knelt by my bed, folded my hands, and started to talk to God aloud. "God, I thank you for this day and for what you have done in my life." I thought that was at least a good start. If only I could keep my momentum up. "I know I am supposed to pray, so here it goes . . ." And I proceeded to provide God with a list of things I needed or wanted in my life. I also gave him my list of people who needed help or intervention in their lives. My prayer became something like a bulleted list. I prayed:

✧ Help me do well in my upcoming tests at school.
✧ Give me direction about where you want me to go to college and what you want me to do with my life.
✧ Heal my sister, who has diabetes.
✧ Help my friend, Kevin, as he tries to serve you.
✧ Bless my youth group and the upcoming outreach we are holding.

Not only did I pray through a bulleted list, but I actually wrote down what I had on my heart to pray about. The list seemed long when I wrote it, but somehow when I was done saying it aloud to God, I had only prayed about ninety seconds. So I tried to come up with other things to say, searching my mind for things that I could possibly ask for and pray about.

The best I could do was fill seven minutes of actual prayer.

I felt a bit ashamed that my time with God was so short and seemed so much less than what I expected it should be. I didn't want to think about how I would answer my youth pastor when he asked about my attempt at this new prayer life. I felt I was obviously either incredibly shallow in my approach to God, or other people understood something about prayer that I didn't.

Good Company

If you've felt this way about prayer, then know you're in good company. In fact, the disciples of Jesus, the people who walked with Him through His ministry, had the same kinds of questions that you and I have about how to approach God in prayer.

In Matthew 6, the disciples basically said to Jesus, "Look we've watched how you talk to your Father in prayer, and we've seen the results of your prayer life. You're obviously doing something different than us. Our prayers lack the impact yours have. Can you teach us how to do this right? Because we feel like we're missing something."

Jesus' response is a famous one!

He taught His disciples what has become known as the Lord's Prayer. A better title for this prayer would probably be the Disciple's Prayer because it was Jesus' recommendation of a pattern that His followers could use in prayer.

Most likely, you know how the prayer goes: "Our Father which art in heaven, hallowed be thy name. Thy kingdom come, Thy will be done in earth, as it is in heaven. Give us this day our daily bread. And forgive us our debts, as we forgive our debtors. And lead us not into temptation, but deliver us from evil: For thine is the kingdom, and the power, and the glory, forever. Amen" (Matthew 6:9–13, KJV).

There's a major misconception concerning these phrases that Jesus used to teach His disciples about prayer. Some have come to believe that Jesus wanted us to repeat these exact words in this exact order, and that by repeating this prayer, we would somehow trigger a response from heaven. So people repeat the prayer, many times, without necessarily thinking about what they are praying.

In reality, this prayer was never intended to be an exercise in memorization and recitation but, rather, a mini-teaching on the various elements involved in effective communication with God. If we take time to slow down and meditate on these words, we discover six main elements involved in prayer.

The Pattern

Worship—"Our Father which art in heaven, hallowed be thy name." With the first line, Jesus set a tone of intimate worship that leads into the rest of the prayer. First, He addressed God as Father. This was a radical concept because no one had addressed God as their father until this moment in history. You might say, "Jesus is the Son of God, of course He would call Him Father." But Jesus showed a radical shift in religious practice by extending the same privilege to everyone by starting the prayer with "*Our* Father."

Jesus then affirmed that our Father rules from heaven and that all things are under His authority. Jesus praised His Father's name by pairing it with the term *hallowed*. The disciples would have understood that the name of a person represented his character.

So we, too, start our prayer time with worship. We are called to recognize who God is, what authority He possesses, how He can be trusted, and who we are in relation to Him. It's all about setting the context for our prayers so that we understand the magnitude of the person we are talking to and the ability He has to do whatever is needed in the world.

✦ We are called to recognize who God is, what authority He possesses, how He can be trusted, and who we are in relation to Him.

Agreement—"Thy kingdom come, Thy will be done in earth, as it is in heaven." After spending time in worship, we need to recognize that our prayers don't start the process of God's action. God is already in motion trying to accomplish good things for us. Instead of just asking for what we think we need, we need to pause and realize that God has a will and purpose for us and for everything going on around us.

We pray for His kingdom to come. So we ask Him to come and rule in our lives and in our world. We invite His leadership. We invite Him to take over in areas where confusion and darkness reign.

We pray for His will to be done. So we ask God to do everything that He wants to do. We agree with God for His will to be released in every area of our lives. (We will spend some time in future chapters discussing how to pray the will of God with confidence.)

Thanksgiving—"Give us this day our daily bread." There are two important aspects of this statement. First, we recognize the "bread" that God has already supplied. This is a moment to pause in gratitude for the things God has already given. So we take time to list all the past provisions.

Before we ask for more bread—we thank God for His goodness in providing the many things that sustain our lives.

Specific Requests—"Give us this day our daily bread." The second application of this statement is to ask God to meet specific needs in our lives. Yes, it's completely okay to ask Him for what you need. Some people have been taught that it's selfish to ask God for things for themselves. Nowhere in the Bible does God tell us *not* to ask for what we need. In fact, in this same passage, Jesus said, "ask and it will be given to you; seek, and you will find; knock, and it will be opened to you" (Matthew 7:7 NKJV).

Confession—"And forgive us our debts, as we forgive our debtors." You can see two applications in this sentence as well. First, we do an inventory of our lives and ask God to forgive us for whatever we might have thought, said, or done that has been offensive to Him.

Second, we choose to forgive those who have offended us in what they have said, done, or attempted to do to us.

Worship—"For thine is the kingdom, and the power, and the glory, forever. Amen." Jesus ended His prayer with a format similar to the beginning of the prayer. After agreeing with God's will, showing gratitude for His blessings, requesting for needs and desires, and confessing the weight of sin, Jesus once again worshipped God. Jesus again recognized the power of God and stated that He is the Ruler of heaven and has authority over all.

What Does This Have to Do with Me?

This prayer guide is designed to follow Jesus' advice about how to approach God in prayer. There's a new pattern every day for you to pray through based on famous prayers in the

Bible. Each day, the various elements from the Lord's Prayer are included in the pattern alongside the outlined format for the day.

Here's how it works.

As you begin your prayer time, the pattern listed for the day will guide you through a strong season of prayer. It will help you know what to say during your time with God and will give you confidence, variety, and effectiveness in your time with Him.

A pattern like this one helped me learn to pray at fifteen years of age. When I told my youth pastor about my frustration regarding prayer, he suggested a simple pattern to pray that was similar to the elements of the Lord's Prayer.

So I knelt down by my bedside. I actually pulled out a watch with a timer and disciplined myself to spend five minutes on each aspect of prayer. Since worship was the first segment, I put a worship song on my tape player (yes I'm old enough to remember cassette tapes), and I sang along. I worshipped God for about five minutes.

I spent the next five minutes agreeing with God for His leadership to come into every area of my life.

Then, I spent five minutes making a list of things I was thankful for. I wrote them down on a sheet of paper in a notebook so I could remember them in future prayer times. After I made the list, I spent another five minutes asking for things that I needed and for the needs of people in my life.

Already, I had spent twenty minutes in prayer.

Finally, I completed the other two aspects. I confessed my sins to God and forgave my offenders. Then I concluded my time with another recorded worship song and songs of praise. It was an awesome time with God. I had spent thirty minutes in prayer and felt great about it.

What a fantastic way to start the day!

My conscience was clean. My heart was right. My spirit was full. The atmosphere of my life was filled with peace. I felt connected to God, and I knew He was walking with me throughout the day.

My hope is that this prayer guide will help you start every day with that kind of momentum. I pray that your confidence will increase as you pray, and that the Holy Spirit will be poured out in your life in His great power.

CHAPTER 2

PRAYING GOD'S WILL

Isn't it interesting that Jesus taught His disciples to pray for the "will of God" to be done? That phrase is so ingrained in our minds we might not stop to think about what it says: "Thy kingdom come, Thy will be done in earth as it is in heaven."

Don't many questions come to mind when you think about that?

- ✧ What is God's will? How am I supposed to know it so I can pray it?
- ✧ If it is God's will, then why is it even necessary for me to ask for it?
- ✧ Can't God just do what He wills to do?
- ✧ Are my prayers even necessary to accomplish God's will?

The next five principles will help to clear up some of these confusing and frustrating questions.

Principle One: God's will doesn't automatically happen on earth! If you look around, you see so many things that are just *not* God's will: abuse, disease, prejudice, hatred, human trafficking, genocide, murder. In fact, we live in a place where God's will does *not* happen most of the time. Think about that for a moment. We live in a place where God's will does *not* happen most of the time.

When God created Adam and Eve, He placed them in the garden of Eden. God's will happened there every day without fail, and it was a perfect place. Heaven is also a perfect place. We know that we will die one day, and if our faith is in Jesus Christ,

15

the Bible promises that we will go to heaven. Heaven is a place where the will of God happens every day all the time.

We live in the season between Eden and heaven.

Adam and Eve chose to do their own will when they ate of the fruit of the Tree of Knowledge of Good and Evil (Genesis 3). Due to those actions, we inherited a world where the will of sinful people and the will of spiritual forces of darkness rule the day. Our world is not a perfect place but a rather painful place.

Principle Two: Our prayers release God's will into our world. "Thy kingdom come, thy will be done in earth, as it is in heaven." Let's reword that line: "May the will of God that is always done in the heavens, be released to take effect on the earth. May the kingdom of God (His rulership and leadership) manifest in my life, my marriage, my family, and my world."

God placed Adam and Eve in the garden and gave them the ability to choose. Even more than that, He gave them authority over the place where they lived. So what happened in the garden was directly determined by whether or not the will of Adam and Eve was aligned with the will of God.

When they chose their own way—they reaped the consequence of pain.

Principle Three: Prayer is the first step in proper realignment with God's will. When we pray, we align our will with God's will. We use our authority as human beings, made in God's image, to engage with and enforce God's will on the earth. When there's a place in our lives or relationships that is filled with pain because it isn't aligned with God's will, our prayers play a part in transforming that situation.

✧ When we pray, we align our will with God's will.

Consider the story of Mary the mother of Jesus. In Luke 1, the angel Gabriel appeared to her and proclaimed that she was going to have a son by the power of the Holy Spirit. He explained that this child would be the Messiah, the Son of God. She objected, of course, because she was a virgin and what the angel told her was logically and naturally impossible. The angel replied, "With God nothing shall be impossible" (Luke 1:37 NKJV).

Then Mary prayed a prayer of alignment. "Let it be to me according to your word" (Luke 1:38 NKJV).

Mary demonstrates what it means to pray the will of God. It's a decision to agree with what God has already said He wants to do. As we agree with God, in prayer, He acts on our behalf. At the moment Mary agreed with God's will in her life, the miracle of conception ignited within her womb.

Principle Four: Effective prayer starts by asking God to do what He already desires to do. First John 5:14–15 (NIV) says, "This is the confidence we have in approaching God: that if we ask anything according to his will, he hears us. And if we know that he hears us—whatever we ask—we know that we have what we asked of him."

Let me use a silly illustration to amplify the above verses. I have five children. Imagine, one of my sons comes to me and makes a request. "Father, would it be ok with you if I go upstairs to my room and clean it?" I can guarantee you that the answer is already yes. Why? It's always the will of Jeff to have his kids clean their rooms.

Doesn't it make sense? If we ask for something that God already wants, He is going to say yes. He isn't going to refuse us if we ask for something that He has already made clear is part of His desired plan. According to 1 John 5, if we ask for what God wants, He hears us. (It's impressive and He hears us.) Not only does He hear us, He responds with a resounding yes!

We so often get prayer backwards. We think that prayer is trying to persuade God to do something He really doesn't want to do, when prayer is actually agreeing with God regarding things He has already willed to do. Martin Luther said this about prayer: "Prayer is not overcoming God's reluctance, but laying hold of His willingness."

Principle Five: When we pray God's Word, we are praying God's will. This prayer guide is designed to aid you in praying things that are God's will. Each of the thirty-one days includes prayers that are biblically based. Since the Holy Spirit inspired the Bible, word for word, we know that He places power on what He wrote. So if we are praying a promise or prayer contained within the Bible, we can be confident we are praying something that aligns with His expressed purpose.

In the next chapter, we will talk about the power of praying the Bible. There is such power that comes into prayer when we aim biblical prayers toward our life situations. Scripture becomes the ammunition that makes prayer effective.

CHAPTER 3

PRAYING GOD'S WORD

Several years ago, Bruce Wilkinson published his bestselling book, *The Prayer of Jabez*. Thousands of people not only purchased this book, but they began praying the pattern of prayer Jabez used when he prayed. Bruce Wilkinson said, "If you were to ask me what sentence—other than my prayer for salvation—has revolutionized my life and ministry the most, I would tell you that it was the cry of a [man] named Jabez, who is still remembered not for what he did, but for what he prayed—and for what happened next."[1]

The Bible summarizes the powerful life of Jabez in just two verses:

> "Jabez was more honorable than his brothers. His mother had named him Jabez, saying, 'I gave birth to him in pain.' Jabez cried out to the God of Israel, 'Oh, that you would bless me and enlarge my territory! Let your hand be with me, and keep me from harm so that I will be free from pain.' And God granted his request" (1 Chronicles 4:9–10 NIV).

Prior to Wilkinson's book, very few people had ever heard of Jabez, who has an obscure mention in the genealogies found in the early part of 1 Chronicles. But these two verses are fascinating based on four elements:

1. **The Name**—Jabez means "pain" or "what a pain!" Can you imagine a mom naming her child What a Pain? Jabez had to overcome the identity of pain that was declared over him by his parents.

2. **The Result**—Jabez was more honorable than his brothers. The word *honorable* means "weighty" or "significant" and "one who carries the respect of others due to the positive impact they bring with them."

3. **The Process**—What made Jabez different? He didn't just accept his lot in life; he cried out to God in prayer. His prayers changed his destiny and reoriented his identity.

4. **The Prayer**—There are five aspects to the prayer of Jabez that become a pattern for us to use in a similar fashion.

> ✧ When we find a prayer recorded in the Bible, we can adopt it for ourselves and apply it in our own prayers.

The prayer of Jabez is a great example of applying biblical prayers to our own lives. The actual words of the Bible and the promises that are outlined are inspired by the breathings of the Holy Spirit. When we find a prayer recorded in the Bible, we can adopt it for ourselves and apply it in our own prayers. The prayer that Jabez offered to God is one we can implement in our own lives.

Jabez made five requests:

✧ Bless me

✧ Enlarge my territory

✧ Let your hand be upon me

✧ Keep me from harm (evil)

✧ Free me from pain (his old identify)

In the last chapter, we learned that the most effective prayer is one that agrees with God's will. When we ask for something God wants, we know He hears and answers that prayer. The easiest way to pray God's will is to pray His Word. When we pray according to the prayers and the promises documented for us in the Bible, we know that we are asking for something God already wants to do.

We pray God's will when we pray the prayers of the Bible. This prayer guide includes many biblical prayers, such as the prayer of Jabez. You can adopt and apply these Holy Spirit-inspired prayers for your own life and family.

We pray God's will when we pray the promises of the Bible. This is what the apostle Paul wrote in 2 Corinthians 1:20, "For no matter how many promises God has made, they are 'Yes' in Christ. And so through him the 'Amen' is spoken by us to the glory of God."

There are several truths about the promises of God:

✧ God has made promises to His people in the Scriptures.

✧ God's will is our inheritance. It's just as if a rich relative has died and has left us a large inheritance that is provided for us in their last will and testament.

✧ When Jesus died on the cross, He said yes to all these promises. The cross ratified or instituted the will of God.

✧ We access all of our inheritance (all of God's promises) when we say amen, which means "so be it" or "I agree."

When we pray, we are agreeing with God's promises. Since the answer is already yes, we are simply enforcing God's will as we come into agreement with His promises. Jesus has already made His intent clear. He said yes when He died on the cross and rose from the grave. Our prayers simply access what Jesus has already provided.

This prayer guide also helps us identify the promises of God so that we can say amen to them as we stand upon them in prayer.

We pray God's will when we pray with the person of the Holy Spirit. Romans 8:26–27 gives us even more insight into praying God's will, "In the same way, the Spirit helps us in our weakness. We do not know what we ought to pray for, but the Spirit himself intercedes for us through wordless groans. And he who searches our hearts knows the mind of the Spirit, because the Spirit intercedes for God's people in accordance with the will of God."

✧ We are weak. We often don't have a clue as to what to pray.

✧ The Holy Spirit lives within us and can help us pray.

✧ The Holy Spirit knows the will of God and helps us pray according to God's will.

It's important to note that prayer is not just reading words on a page. Yes, this prayer guide includes Bible verses, promises, and prayers from the Bible. You can read them aloud to God as you agree with them in prayer. But prayer is so much more than just reciting promises and prayers.

As you pray, remember that the Holy Spirit wants to pray with you and through you. As you pray, you may feel an inner sense of burden or heaviness about a situation or a person in need. Sometimes, you don't even need words to pray. God's Word says that you can "groan" out of your spirit and He understands.

In fact, the Holy Spirit will often groan along with you. As the Holy Spirit groans and cries within you, there is a spiritual connection between you and God—between heaven and earth, between the Holy Spirit within you and God the Father who hears your cry.

God wants you to pray effectively. He wants you to pray confidently. He wants your prayers to make an impact. He has equipped you with His Word and with His Spirit so that when you pray, you aren't just making wishes to God. He wants your prayers to be in agreement with His will and purpose. He wants your prayers to release the resources of heaven and bring them to fruition in situations on the earth.

CHAPTER 4

LET'S GET PRACTICAL

Now that we've reviewed the importance of prayer, let's take a few minutes to deal with some practical components of developing a consistent habit of personal time with God.

Bill Hybels talks about the key to developing a new habit. He calls the practice "advanced decision making," which is the ability to make an appointment or plan in advance in order to stick to it:

> The essence of discipline, then, is delayed gratification, and the key to practicing discipline is "advanced decision making." When you come to the point in your spiritual life of saying, "I'm going to harness the power of discipline to commit myself to meeting my minimum requirements," you are really saying to yourself and to God, "I'll do whatever it takes. I'm willing to go through the discomfort and pain of the investment stage first so that I can experience the blessedness of flourishing as a Christian for the rest of my life. I'm willing to set up a structure that will ensure my success." That's discipline.[2]

Spending daily time with God requires some strong proactive decisions.

Set a Daily Appointment

I'm much more likely to follow through with a daily prayer time, if I've thought through when I'm going to slot this into my day. So I ask myself, "What time of day can I most consistently set aside thirty minutes to be alone with God?"

For most of us, that's the early morning hours. Set your alarm thirty minutes earlier than normal. Get up and devote the first part of your day to God. To be honest, I hated this advice when someone gave it to me because I'm not an early morning person. I do my best thinking late at night. So I tried having my prayer time thirty minutes before I went to bed.

While for some people this is a viable option, I just couldn't be as consistent with late night appointments with God. There were social occasions or family interruptions that made this option more inconsistent. The other benefit of starting the day in prayer is that it has a powerful effect upon my demeanor and approach to the rest of the day. When I start the day with God, I feel better about everything.

Jesus started the day off with His Father. Mark 1:35 says, "Very early in the morning, while it was still dark, Jesus got up, left the house and went off to a solitary place, where he prayed."

Whether it's early in the morning or on a lunch-break or late in the evening, it's important to set an appointment with God and then work to keep that appointment every day. The specific time or place you choose are not important as long as they work for you. What is important is the intimacy you'll gain from these special times with God.

Set a Place for Prayer

We just read that Jesus "went off to a solitary place where he prayed." He escaped the noise and the chaos of real life and created a quiet setting for His intimate moments with God.

Is there a place where you will have quiet and uninterrupted moments alone with God? This may be a huge challenge for you. It was for me when my kids were younger. Melodie and I have five children and at one point they were all under the age of seven. It was rare that there would ever be even a single quiet place in our home at any time!

John Wesley's mom, Suzanna, had nineteen kids! She raised an incredible family; two of her boys became great world leaders and tremendous men of God. John became the leader of the Methodist revival, and Charles became one of the great hymn writers of the church in the 1700s. Suzanna couldn't find a quiet place in her home to pray, so she would go into the kitchen and cover her face with her apron. Her children learned not to bother Mom when she was having her time alone with God in the kitchen. Suzanna knew the importance of her time with God and went to whatever lengths it took to keep that appointment. Surely you, too, can find a place to have time alone with God!

This is another reason why early in the morning is often best. When my kids were small, I would gete up at 5 a.m. and have my prayer time. Then I would often go back to sleep for an hour before I went to work.

Set a Plan for Your Prayer Time

I recommend that you start your time with God by reading a portion of the Bible. I begin my time with God by reading in the *One Year Bible* (check it out at oneyearbibleonline.com). It takes me about ten minutes to read the assigned portion for the day. If I read the assigned portion every day, I will have read the entire Bible in one year.

Shorter Bible reading plans are available on a website/app called youversion.com. You can choose from a variety of reading plans and versions of the Bible that are easy to read and understand.

After completing your time of Bible reading, pull out this prayer guide and pray one of the patterns in this book. There are more than one month's worth of prayer patterns available to you here.

If you spend ten minutes reading the Bible and twenty minutes in prayer, you will have a strong start to a consistent and meaningful prayer life.

✧ If you spend thirty minutes a day with God, you'll never ever regret it.

Expect Powerful Results

One of the greatest things I've ever done for my life, my marriage, and my ministry was to follow the advice I've just given to you. If you spend thirty minutes a day with God, you'll never ever regret it. My prayer time enhanced all areas of my life. The intimate relationship that I cultivated with God brought many positive changes to my life:

✧ **My attitude improved.** My tendency is to be irritable and angry. But when I'm connected to God, I feel so much more peace and live with grace and patience.

✧ **My relationships grew.** Because I had peace on the inside, I was able to walk in peace on the outside. My wife can tell you that I'm a much better man when I have had my time with God. I'm able to interact with the people in my life in a transformed way simply because I connect with God daily.

✧ **My wisdom increased.** Reading the Bible daily has given me a perspective on life that benefits me in every way. For instance, I'm a much better dad because of the wisdom I've gained. My leadership within the organizations I oversee is also much stronger with a heightened perspective.

✧ **My life became more fruitful.** So many positive things are happening in my life that can only be explained as favors from heaven or answers to prayer.

✧ **My temptations decreased.** If my heart is filled with peace, I no longer feel the magnetism toward selfish or self-destructive behaviors.

✧ **My confidence grew.** I have boldness about my relationship with God and a confidence that I know how to pray when needs arise in my life or in the world around me.

✧ **My relationship with God grew stronger.** I feel like I'm actually in a relationship. I know God. He knows me. I am walking every day with the Creator of the universe. He is my friend. I consult Him. I feel His presence. I understand His heart. And I can tell you that it's awesome.

I'm so eager for you to experience these same results. That's why I designed these prayer patterns. I pray that God would bless your time with Him in a mighty way and that you would grow to know Him and His power as it is released into your world.

CHAPTER 5

EXTRA CREDIT

I would like to share three activities that can help you develop an even more intimate prayer life and a deeper relationship with God. These three things will move your prayer life beyond the basics steps we have shared thus far; but don't feel pressured to implement all of them right away. Take your time. Establish your set time, set place, and start to use your Bible reading plan and prayer patterns. When you feel ready to stretch yourself a bit more, consider these "extra credit" activities.

1. Keep a Record of Answered Prayer

You'll find some blank pages in the back of this book that are designed to help you record answered prayers. Some prayers will take years to receive an answer, while others may be answered as soon the words leave your mouth. Document these answered prayers!

Sometimes we're tempted to accuse God of not answering our prayers. Sometimes we concentrate only on the prayers that have yet to be answered, and we forget the many ways that God provides for us each and every day.

When you keep record of answered prayers, you'll find that God does much more in your life than you give Him credit for. When you keep a record of answered prayers over a long period of time, you will be amazed at what you can trace through God's answers. Remembering what God has done can be an incredible source of encouragement.

2. Start a Journal

For over twenty-five years, I've kept a journal. You may be wondering what a journal is and how it differs from a diary. A diary is a record of personal events and feelings. It documents the events of your day and your dealings with life. A journal, however, is a record of what God reveals to you as you study His Word and spend time with Him in prayer.

Here's what I do when I journal:

1. I limit my writing to one page per day so that it never feels overwhelming or burdensome to me.
2. I use a notebook with 5.5 x 8.5 inch paper.
3. My focus for writing is based on a pattern that is recommended by Wayne Cordiero in his book, *The Divine Mentor*.[3] He recommends using a method for journaling called SOAP.

The four elements of SOAP are:

- ✧ **S—Scripture:** I select a verse or two of the Bible and write that text at the top of the page.
- ✧ **O—Observation:** I reflect on what the verse meant at the time it was written to those for whom it was written.
- ✧ **A—Application:** After getting a sense of what the verse meant to the original audience, I then consider what it means for me at this moment.
- ✧ **P—Prayer:** Once I have applied the text to my life situations, I write a sentence or two as a prayer to God regarding the truths I have learned.[4]

3. Find a Prayer Partner or Join a Small Group

The final thing I will recommend is that you connect with a small group or at least a prayer partner. Jesus said, "Again, truly I tell you that if two of you on earth agree about anything they ask for, it will be done for them by my Father in heaven. For where two or three gather in my name, there am I with them" (Matthew 18:19–20).

Several things happen when we agree with others in prayer:

- ✧ **Greater results:** Jesus indicates that the impact of two or more agreeing with God's will is greater than just one praying.

- ✧ **Increased presence:** Praying together with others increases the presence of God in our midst.

- ✧ **Contagious faith:** The faith of others rubs off on you. Your skill as a person of prayer grows. When you are low in faith, others are there to lift you up and vice versa.

A number of years ago, I watched as my wife, Melodie, grew in her prayer life. She joined a small group of women who met every Monday night. Some of these women had been praying with power for years, and their faith and skill rubbed off on Mel. Through the gathering of prayer warriors, she became a prayer force to be reckoned with.

Some things are better caught than taught. Some things we learn best by watching and doing than by listening to a teacher. Prayer is one of those skills. It's not enough to know about it. It's not enough to read about it. The only way you become effective in prayer is to do it.

It's time to get busy!

I pray that God will use these prayer patterns to broaden, deepen, and sharpen your prayer life so that you will experience major breakthroughs as you seek His face.

31 Days
of Prayer

DAY 1

PRAYING THROUGH THE LORD'S PRAYER
(MATTHEW 6:9–13)

How to Begin: Read each line of each segment below in prayer. Then, pause and add some of your own thoughts. Amplify each sentence with more things that come to mind.

Read: Matthew 6:9–13

Praise: "Our Father which art in heaven, hallowed be thy name."

- ✧ I praise You for who You are (my Father, the Creator, my Savior).
- ✧ I recognize that You rule from heaven and have authority over everything that is happening on the earth.
- ✧ I praise Your name. (You are loving, merciful, faithful, powerful, gracious, compassionate, etc.)

Agreement: "Thy kingdom come, Thy will be done in earth, as it is in heaven."

- ✧ May Your kingdom come in my life (may You rule over my thoughts, words, and choices).
- ✧ May Your will be done in me (in my life, in my family, in my work, in my trials, in all areas of my life).
- ✧ May Your kingdom come and Your will be done in my small group, in my church, in my community, and in this nation.

✧ May all of the good things that are stored up in Your will (all Your promises that You have already said yes to in Christ) be released in my life (see 2 Corinthians 1:19–20).

Requests: "Give us this day our daily bread."

✧ I thank You for the way You have provided for my needs.

✧ I specifically thank You for (name things you are thankful for).

✧ God, what I need today is (list specific needs and requests).

✧ God, I ask you to (list specific needs that others have and pray for God to provide what is needed).

(In the back of this prayer guide you will find a place to list needs and record the way God answers your prayers.)

Confession: "Forgive us our debts, as we forgive our debtors."

✧ I confess my sin (list specifics), and I ask You to forgive me for (specific sin).

✧ I thank You that You have chosen to forgive me. I declare that if we confess our sins, You are *"faithful and just and will forgive us our sins and purify us from all unrighteousness"* (see 1 John 1:9).

✧ I choose to forgive anyone who has offended me: I choose to forgive (list the person's name) and I release them from their offense toward me."

Declaration: "Lead us not into temptation, but deliver us from evil."

✧ I declare that Jesus Christ has defeated the Devil on my behalf. I am an overcomer through Christ!

✧ I pray a hedge of protection around me, my family, and all those under my care.

✧ God, help me see where I'm vulnerable to temptation today, and give me the strength to overcome.

✦ I choose to flee from sin and take my stand and fight against the Devil.

✦ Holy Spirit, fill my life and give me the power and the satisfaction in God to say no to sin and yes to God.

Praise: "For Thine is the kingdom, and the power, and the glory, forever. Amen."

✦ Yours is the kingdom—You rule over all.

✦ Yours is the power—nothing is too hard for You.

✦ Yours is the glory—may my life bring honor to You today. Amen.

DAY 2

PRAYING THE PRAYER OF JABEZ

Read: 1 Chronicles 4:9–10

Begin With Praise:

- ✧ I declare that God is the One who spoke the world into being.
- ✧ He speaks and things are created and sustained.
- ✧ Read aloud Psalm 29.
- ✧ I declare that nothing is impossible for God, and nothing is too hard for God. He is able to do all things.
- ✧ I declare that God is the Author and Perfector of my life and of my faith. He completes the good work He starts (see Hebrews 12:1–3).
- ✧ Read aloud Philippians 1:6.

Request #1: "Oh, that you would bless me . . ."

- ✧ May the same God who spoke the world into existence speak His favor over my life. Breath of God, come breathe on me.
- ✧ May You bless (speak favor over) my family.
- ✧ May You breathe Your favor on our health, our home, and our finances. Make us so blessed that we overflow and become a blessing to others (see Genesis 12:1–3).

Request #2: ". . . and enlarge my territory!"

- ✧ God, just as the people of Israel had an inheritance (of land) in the Promised Land, so I have an inheritance in your kingdom. Lord, help me to know the hope of my calling, the riches of my inheritance (as your child), and the surpassing great power for me as I believe (see Ephesians 1:18).

✧ Enlarge my vision to see what You have in mind for my life.

✧ Enlarge my heart of compassion for people.

✧ Enlarge my territory and make me a great influence to expand Your kingdom. (Pray this for loved ones, your church, small group, and pastor: "Lord may you enlarge their territory.")

Request #3: "Let Your hand be with me . . ."

✧ Establish me in every way: my life, my work, my relationships, and my ministry. Establish the work of my hands.

✧ Let Your hand of healing be on my life and on those who need Your touch today. (Pray for specific healing needs.)

✧ Let Your hand of provision be released in my life and in those who need Your breakthrough today. (Pray for specific needs of provision.)

✧ Let Your hand be upon my loved ones (name specific people).

Request #4: "Keep me from harm . . ."

✧ Rebuke the Devil on my behalf and on behalf of all those under my care and authority.

✧ Free me from any sinful habit, hurtful words, and un-Christ-like attitudes.

✧ I repent and ask for Your forgiveness and for freedom in my life.

✧ Lord, send Your angels before me to defeat any spiritual attack and to establish Your will for my life.

Request #5: "Free me from all pain."

✧ Lord, just as Jabez didn't accept his old identity, I throw off the identity of my past and declare that

I'm a new creation in Christ Jesus—the old has gone and the new has come (see 2 Corinthians 5:16–17).

✧ I declare that I'm now a child of God, His workmanship created in Christ Jesus for good works, which He has prepared in advance for me to do (see Ephesians 2:10).

✧ I also choose to forsake any pain-causing actions (see list in Colossians 3:5–10). I die to my old ways and choose to put on Christ as my new way of life (see Colossians 3:1–4)

✧ God has given me a destiny of blessing and not of pain. I declare the blessing of Abraham in my life. I pray that those who bless me will be blessed, and those who curse me will be cursed. And may all the peoples on earth be blessed through my life (see Genesis 12:1–3).

DAY 3

PRAYING THE TEN COMMANDMENTS

Background: In Deuteronomy 5, we have record of the Ten Commandments that Moses received from God for the people of Israel. These commandments are not just rules; they represent God's character and nature. They represent God's best for our lives. Each of these prayers below corresponds to the commandments.

Read: Deuteronomy 5:1–22

Command #1: God, I place You on the throne of my life as the only One I will worship. I recognize that my choice to worship You exclusively is the only path to true intimacy with You. I want to know You in an intimate and powerful way. I say yes to Your proposal in commandment number one: I will have no other gods before You.

Suggestion: Spend some moments in worship (use a worship CD, read a psalm).

Command #2: God, I choose today to worship You in spirit and in truth, I know that Jesus is the radiance of Your glory and the exact representation of Your nature (Hebrews 1:1–3). So I declare my allegiance to the person of Jesus as my way to God, the truth, and the only way to life (see John 14:6).

Suggestion: Select one of the qualities of Jesus, and ask God to help you become more like Jesus in that way.

Command #3: God, I don't want to do anything that would grieve Your Spirit. Convict me of any words, actions, attitudes, thoughts, or motives that are pushing You out of my life (see Ephesians 4:25–5:10).

Suggestion: Confess any sin and ask God for His forgiveness through Christ.

Command #4: God, I choose to give You my time and my life today. As I take this time for prayer, I ask You to help me to rest in You. Replenish my soul, and help my life to be refocused on Your purpose.

Suggestion: Think for a moment about how you are spending your time. Ask God to help you prioritize properly.

Command #5: God, I recognize Your desire to provide me with a long and prosperous life. I choose to have an attitude of honor toward the sources of authority You have placed in my life. I choose to honor:

✧ Your Word and I ask You to open my eyes to the truth of the Scriptures.

✧ My parents (pray for God's blessing on them today).

✧ My spouse (if applicable).

✧ My boss.

✧ Government leaders.

Commands #6–9: God, I ask You to make me a person of integrity and wholeness. I ask You to reveal to me any area of compromise in my life:

✧ Have you taken anything that is not yours? Choose to confess it and make restitution.

✧ Are you harboring anger or bitterness? Choose to forgive and ask God to heal your heart.

✧ Are you participating in sexual sin? Turn from it and ask God for forgiveness.

✧ Have you been dishonest in any way? Go back and set the record straight with anyone you may have misled.

✧ Have you said anything hurtful about or to anyone? Ask God to forgive you and consider how you might make this right.

✧ Have you done anything hurtful to someone else? Ask God to forgive you and consider how you might make this right.

Command #10: God, I recognize that my satisfaction and success in life are based on Your favor, not on what I can accomplish or acquire. Forgive me for coveting what You have not yet provided for me.

Declare: I believe that I can be content right now. You, God, are the "I AM" and are present with me with more than enough joy and provision for the moment I am in. I choose joy.

I choose to be thankful for what You have provided (list those things).

I choose to rest in Your goodness for me right now. I don't have to wait to be content. I choose to enjoy Your presence and provision in my life right now.

DAY 4

PRAYING MIRACLES IN THE BOOK OF JOHN

Background: There are seven miracles recorded for us in the book of John. Each story is a sign (a miracle with a message) designed to strengthen our faith in Jesus' identity. Before each prayer segment, you may want to read the miracle story to feed your faith.

Miracle 1: Water Into Wine (Overcoming Disappointment—John 2:1-12)

✧ I declare Jesus as the Creator of the universe and as Master over the elements of nature. He can speak and things are created and transformed. (The Creator)

✧ I declare Jesus as the source of "the best wine" and of true fulfillment and lasting satisfaction in my life. (The Satisfier)

✧ I declare that His blood is the only true cleansing for my sin. I rejoice in the finished work of the cross. (My Redeemer)

Miracle 2: Speaking Healing (Overcoming Doubt—John 4:43-54)

✧ Jesus, in John 4:50, You spoke the word and healing came to a dying child. I ask You to speak healing in the following people today (list people who have physical needs).

✧ Lord, I choose to have confidence in Your Word, for faith comes by hearing and hearing by the Word of God (Romans 10:17). I choose to put my trust in what You have said and not what I feel or see.

Miracle 3: Acting In Faith (Overcoming Disability— John 5:1–15)

✧ Lord, You told the man beside the pool of Bethesda, to do what he could not naturally do (pick up his mat and walk). As he obeyed in faith, the miracle occurred. Lord, what is it that You want me to do today? Speak to me, and I will obey in faith. (Take a few minutes to listen to God.)

✧ Jesus, I believe you are able to do the impossible. I pray for (list a name or situation) and that you would reverse the situation and do a miracle of provision in their life.

✧ Lord, may You be glorified in every situation. May people come to see the risen Jesus through the miracles that You perform in my world.

Miracle 4: Feeding the 5,000 (Overcoming Unmet Desire—John 6:1–13)

✧ Lord, just as You multiplied the five loaves and two fish to feed thousands, so I offer my life and my resources to You. Multiply what I place in Your hands, not only to meet my needs, but to give me enough to share.

✧ I also declare that You are able to meet the needs of my local church and other ministries and missionaries. (List specific ministries.)

✧ I declare that You are able to provide for the poor of my city and of the world. Use me to make a difference. Give me resources, creativity, connections, and opportunity.

✧ Lord, with You there will always be more than enough. I choose to be content under Your care today. I thank You for the many ways You have provided for me already. (List things you are thankful for.)

Miracle 5: Walking On Water (Overcoming Despair—John 6:16–24)

✧ Lord, just as You came to the disciples in the middle of the storm, I believe You are present with me in my trial today. Help me see You in my storm.

✧ Lord, you see how (name a person in a storm) needs Your presence with what they are going through. Reveal Yourself to them today.

✧ As long as Peter kept his eyes on You, he was able to walk on water. When he put his focus on the wind and the waves, he began to sink. I choose to fix my eyes on You and to rest in Your ability to see me through.

Miracle 6: Healing a Man Born Blind (Overcoming Darkness—John 9)

✧ Lord, open the eyes of those who live in spiritual darkness and cause them to see the light of the gospel of Jesus Christ. I pray for friends and loved ones who need Jesus Christ.

✧ I also pray that You, O Lord, would lift the darkness over my neighborhood, workplace, city, and nation.

Miracle 7: Raising of Lazarus (Overcoming Death—John 11)

✧ Jesus, I declare You as the Victor over death. You are the resurrection and the life. As I believe in You, even when I die, I know I will continue to live. Thank You for the promise of eternal life.

✧ I praise You because nothing is too hard for You. You can take the things that have died and resurrect them in my world.

DAY 5

PRAYING THE A-C-T-S PRAYERS

Background: This prayer pattern has four segments that are easy to remember: A-C-T-S. Take five to ten minutes on each segment as you pray through today.

A-doration (choose a praise/worship option)

- ✧ Listen to some worship music.
- ✧ Read Psalm 139 aloud.
- ✧ Declare who God is to you: "God, I declare that you are . . ."
  - · Creator
  - · Sustainer
  - · Savior
  - · Redeemer
  - · Lover
  - · Healer
  - · Friend
  - · Lord/Master

(Example: I thank You God that You are the sustainer of my life. It is by Your grace that I exist, I breathe, I have the capacity to live and overcome. I declare Your sustaining power in my life.)

C-onfession

"Search me, God, and know my heart; test me and know my anxious thoughts. See if there is any offensive way in me and lead me in the way everlasting" (Psalm 139:23–24).

- ✧ Do an inventory of your life, repent, and seek God's forgiveness:
- ✧ Have you spoken *any words* that were hurtful, critical, doubtful, or ungrateful? Ask forgiveness for these idle words and determine to make them right.

✧ Have you harbored impure, anxious, or harsh *thoughts*? Ask forgiveness for them, renounce them, and take them captive in His name.

✧ Have you had *selfish motives*? Surrender them to God and make it your primary goal to please Him.

✧ Have you had a *poor attitude*? Confess it as sin and choose to have the attitude of Christ.

✧ Have you *acted in disobedience* or rebellion against God? Confess it as sin and choose obedience.

✧ God, I thank You for Your complete forgiveness and for a fresh start today!

T-hanksgiving

✧ Make a list of the earthly benefits that God has provided for you. (Write them down on one of the pages in the back of this book.)

✧ Make a list of all the spiritual blessings that you have in Christ. Thank Him for all He has done for you.

✧ "God, please help me develop and live out of a grateful heart."

S-eek (make requests)

✧ Ask God for the things you need today. Be specific.

✧ Ask God for the things you want today. Be specific.

✧ Ask God for the specific things that are needed in the lives of those around you (options listed below):
  · Family
  · Friends who need Christ
  · Pastors/church needs
  · Small Group needs
  · National needs
  · Missions needs
  · Workplace needs

Praise: Conclude your prayer time by expressing in your own words what you love and value about God.

DAY 6

PRAYING THE PROMISES OF GOD

Background: Today, we are going to focus our prayers on some of the great promises in the Bible, and we are going to agree with them and aim them specifically toward our lives and our families.

Praise and Thanksgiving: Read Psalm 103 aloud.

- ✧ Thank You for forgiving all of my sins.
- ✧ Thank You for healing me and providing me with health.
- ✧ Thank You for redeeming my life from the things that held me captive (list them specifically).
- ✧ Thank You for crowning my life with Your unfailing, unconditional love.
- ✧ Thank You for the many good things (list them specifically) with which you have satisfied my life.

Confession:

- ✧ I declare the words that Jesus said on the cross: "It is finished." I receive the finished work of Christ in my life. Nothing more can be added to what He has done. He completed the work. Now I am forgiven and accepted by God.
- ✧ I declare that I overcome the Devil and every attack against my life (Revelation 12:11) by the blood of the Lamb (the finished work of Christ on the cross) and by the word of my own testimony. I declare that today is a day of great victory in my life.
- ✧ I declare (Isaiah 54:17) that no weapon formed against me will prosper. I will refute every attack against me, and I will walk in my heritage as a servant of the Lord.

✧ I declare that God has plans for me (Jeremiah 29:11) to prosper me and not to harm me, to give me a future and a hope. I declare that God will reveal Himself to me as I seek Him with all my heart.

Pray for Your Family:

✧ I pray (based on Psalm 112) that God would make my children/grandchildren mighty in the land, that they, as the generation of the upright, would be blessed. May wealth and riches be in their house, and may their righteousness endure forever. Surely, they will never be shaken. They will have no fear of bad news, for their hearts will be steadfast, trusting in the Lord.

✧ I pray (based on Zechariah 2:5) that God would be a Wall of Fire (of protection) around my family and the glory of God would rest upon and within them.

✧ I pray for my family members that You would bless them, enlarge their territory, let your hand be upon them, deliver them from evil, and free them from any pain (1 Chronicles 4:9–10).

Pray for Those Who Need Christ:

✧ According to John 16, I pray that You would convict my friends/family (name them specifically) of sin, and the righteousness available through Christ, and the judgment to come. I pray that they would respond to this awareness by choosing to surrender their lives to Christ.

✧ According to 2 Corinthians 4:4, I pray that You would open their blinded eyes and reveal the person of Jesus Christ to them.

Pray for Those in Authority: (spiritual leaders, employers, government officials)

✧ I pray (based on 3 John 2) that they may prosper and be in health and that even their soul would prosper.

✧ I pray that they would govern with wisdom and grace so that we might live peaceful and quiet lives in all godliness and holiness (see 1 Timothy 2:2).

For Your Nation:

✧ "If My people who are called by my name, will humble themselves and pray, and seek my face and turn from their wicked ways, then will I hear from heaven, and I will forgive their sin and heal their land" (2 Chronicles 7:14). God, may You do this for our nation.

✧ I pray that God would lead the people of this nation to repent and turn to Him—that their sins might be wiped out and times of refreshing might come (see Acts 3:19).

DAY 7

DAY OF PRAISE

Background: Set aside some moments just to worship, as a time when you don't ask God for anything. Just look to spend time in His presence.

Praise: Do one or more of the following:
- ✧ Read aloud 3 or 4 psalms to God.
- ✧ Confess aloud the qualities of God that you are thankful for (holy, all-powerful, all-knowing, loving, merciful, everywhere present, eternal, just, fatherly, unchanging, consistent, dependable).

Worship: Listen to some worship music and take some time to worship to several songs. (Lift your hands or get on your knees—make some physical expression of worship.)

Meditation: Think about a Bible passage you have read recently. Ask the Holy Spirit to reveal to you something from His Word today. (Maybe make an attempt at journaling—see chapter 5 at the beginning of this book.)

Concluding Declarations: I declare that . . .
- ✧ Today I'm not just going to survive, I'm going to overcome and conquer (Romans 8:31–39).
- ✧ God has forgiven my sin and He accepts me completely through Christ (1 John 1:9).
- ✧ Satisfaction isn't found in self-seeking behavior but in the presence of God and in the pursuit of righteous relationships.
- ✧ I'm the temple of the Holy Spirit and God wants to do miracles in my life today (1 Corinthians 6:19–20).

✦ No weapon formed against me can prevail. Today will be a day of victory. I will refute every attack against me and will walk in my full inheritance as a servant of the Lord (Isaiah 54:17).

✦ I can do all things through Christ who gives me strength (Philippians 4:13).

Ask: Lord, would You fill me with the Holy Spirit today? I invite You, Holy Spirit, to overwhelm me so that You might birth good fruit in me (see Galatians 5:22–23).

Use this space to list blessings and praises to God:

DAY 8

PRAYING THE FIVE PURPOSES

Background: There are five purposes that God has for His church and for the life of every believer. We find these five purposes in the Great Commandment (Matthew 22:37–39) and in the Great Commission (Matthew 28:18–20). God's purposes are an expression of God's will. So we can pray with confidence for all five to be accomplished in our world.[5]

Purpose #1: I was planned for God's pleasure (worship).

Declare the following:

✧ Jesus, my life is centered on You—so I choose to worship You.

✧ My purpose in life is to please You in every word and every deed.

✧ I choose to put You on the throne of my heart—I will worship You exclusively. Nothing else compares to You.

✧ I praise Your name, and I want to dwell in Your presence.

✧ Read aloud Psalm 27.

✧ Sing a worship song to God.

Purpose #2: I was formed for God's family (fellowship).

✧ God, I ask You to provide leadership for my family today. I ask You to do the following (name specific things) in my family's life.

✧ God, I ask You to rule and reign over my small group and my local church family. (Pray for specific needs for people in your church and group.)

✧ God, I ask You to bless my pastors with wisdom and revelation and with victory over every spiritual attack. Please give them and their families health and spiritual prosperity in every way.

✧ God, I ask you to send revival to the church in my nation.

Purpose #3: I was created to become like Christ (discipleship).

✧ **Declare:** I thank You, God, that You can use my difficulties to build my life. I choose joy in the midst of my trial (James 1:2–4) and ask You to use my hardships to make me mature and complete, not lacking anything.

✧ **Confess:** God, reveal to me where my life doesn't measure up to the character of Christ. Show me any hurtful words that I have spoken. Reveal to me bad attitudes that need to change. Help me see the poor decisions or sinful habits of my life. Please forgive me. I choose to place every sin under your blood, and I declare that I am forgiven and free.

Purpose #4: I was shaped for service (ministry).

✧ Lord, open my eyes to the needs of hurting people all around me today. I offer myself as an instrument of ministry to those You want me to serve today.

✧ God, give me a servant's heart in my home and in my workplace.

✧ Lord, reveal to me how You want to use me. Help me to see the grace that has been poured into my life (in the areas of pain and struggle—where You have helped me). Help me to share the grace that I have been given with others (see 2 Corinthians 1:9).

✧ Lord, make me aware of what You want me to give in terms of time, talent, or treasure (money) to the needs of the sick, hurting, poor, or lost in the world around me. All that I have is Yours. O Lord, use me.

Purpose #5: I was made for mission (evangelism).

✧ God, I ask You to bring the following three friends/ family members to salvation. (List at least three people who need Christ.)

✧ I pray for the glory of the Lord to fill and overflow my neighborhood and my city. As the waters cover the sea, may Your glory cover this region so that eyes would be opened and people could see the truth that would set them free.

✧ I pray for ministries or missionaries (be specific— name those you know). God, bless them with health, provision, wisdom, revelation, and with laborers for their ministry.

✧ I pray that You would send revival and spiritual breakthrough to the nation/region where these leaders serve.

DAY 9

PRAYING THE PERSON AND WORK OF JESUS

Background: When we want to know what God is like, all we have to do is look at Jesus (Hebrews 1:3). When we want to know what God's will is, all we have to do is look at what Jesus did while here on earth. So we will pray accordingly.

Praise: Recognize the wonderful qualities of Jesus Christ.

- ✧ Jesus, I speak to You right now as a person and a friend. I want You to know that I admire who You are and want to be just like You.
- ✧ Jesus, thank You that You are positive, grace-filled, forgiving, compassionate, and strong.
- ✧ I admire the fact that You are able to believe in me even when I fail and that You never give up on me.
- ✧ Thank You that You delight in me. Your joy is infectious. Help me share Your joy today.
- ✧ Help me to know more of what You are like. Jesus, You are very real. Walk beside me today. Prove Yourself to me in supernatural ways.
- ✧ I declare that You still work miracles in the world today. Demonstrate Your power in my life and in my family.

(What is the most miraculous thing that God could do in your sphere of influence today? Why don't you pray the biggest prayer you can pray today?)

Repentance: Jesus, I choose to be like You.

- ✧ **Attitude:** Lord, reveal to me where I have not shared Your demeanor. Forgive me for a poor attitude. I choose to have the attitude of Christ.

✧ **Words:** Lord, forgive me for speaking words that do not align with Your Word (words of gossip, doubt, insult, pain). Forgive me for when my words sound more like the Devil than like Jesus. I choose to speak faith, blessing, and life.

✧ **Habits/Actions:** Lord, I turn from any activity that I would not feel comfortable doing if You were physically present with me. I choose to live in a way that is becoming to You. I welcome You to walk with me through every part of this day.

Enforce the Victory of the Cross: Read Isaiah 53 Out Loud

✧ Jesus, You carried our **sickness** when You died on the cross. By Your stripes we are healed. I declare the healing power of the cross over the following people (list those who need a physical healing and include yourself if you need a touch).

✧ Jesus, You carried our **sorrows** when You died on the cross. By Your stripes we are healed. I declare Your healing power for those who are dealing with emotional pain (pray for specific individuals). Release Your peace and provision in their lives.

✧ Jesus, You carried our **sins** when You died on the cross. By Your stripes we are healed. I declare Your salvation for those who need to be saved (pray for specific people who need salvation).

✧ I declare Your deliverance over those who are bound in addiction and the habits of sin, and for those who have fallen away from You—that You would draw them back to You (name specific people who need this today).

✧ I declare that You, Jesus, have defeated the Devil and that every enemy is placed under Your feet (disease, death, the Devil). You are risen from the grave. You conquered death and are seated at the right hand of the Father.

✧ You have declared that I share in your victory because I belong to You. You have given me the authority I need to overcome. So I declare Your overcoming power in my life.

✧ I declare that you will place a hedge of protection around my life and:
- My family (anyone under my care)
- My small group
- My local church family
- My pastor(s)
- Others

Praise: I declare that You, Jesus, are the ruler of my life and the ruler over the entire universe. You are the King of Kings—Yours is the kingdom, power, and glory forever.

DAY 10

PRAYING PSALM 23

Background: One of the most beloved psalms, this one was written by David, a shepherd who reflected on how God cares for us in a way similar to how shepherds care for their sheep. Each of these six verses contains a powerful promise. Pray through these promises.

Praise: *"The Lord is my shepherd . . ."*

  ✧ I thank You, Lord, for Your attentive care toward me: for protecting me from predators, for directing me toward provision, and for keeping me from all harm.

  ✧ Lord, You are the Good Shepherd because You loved me enough to lay down Your life for me as one of Your sheep. Thank You for sacrificing Yourself for my redemption and salvation.

  ✧ Thank You that You are committed to my well-being and to my destiny.

Thanksgiving: *"I lack nothing."*

  ✧ Thank God for the many ways He has provided for your life. Try to list as many things as you can think of and thank Him for each one of those provisions in your life.

Requests: *"He makes me lie down in green pastures; he leads me beside quiet waters, he refreshes my soul."*

  ✧ God, You are able to restore what has been destroyed by sin and by Satan. May You do a work of restoration in my world. (List specific areas of your life, your family, or in the lives of those you love.)

"He guides me along the right paths for his name's sake."

✧ Lord, may You guide me today in the paths of righteousness. I ask You to forgive me for wandering from that path in the past. (Repent of specific sins and ask for His cleansing and forgiveness.) I choose to live for Your name's sake (for Your pleasure and Your glory).

"Even though I walk through the darkest valley, I will fear no evil, for You are with me; your rod and your staff, they comfort me."

✧ Lord, I declare that my trust is in You. I refuse to walk in fear. I choose rather to declare that You will lead me through!

✧ I give You permission to discipline me with Your rod and staff and direct my life in how You would like to lead it. I invite You to reveal Your direction to me and to convict my heart of any word, attitude, or decision that is not pleasing to You.

"You prepare a table before me in the presence of my enemies."

✧ May You put a hedge of protection around my life, my family, my small group, my church, and all those under my care. And may You provide Your abundant provision for us today.

✧ I declare Your favor in my life. Rebuke the Devil on our behalf.

"You anoint my head with oil; my cup overflows."

✧ Lord, just as a shepherd used oil to ward off flies and pests, may You keep my life and those under my care free from the unnecessary harassments of the enemy.

✧ God, I declare your protection, provision, and direction over the lives of those who are leaders in this world. (Pray for the following by name.)

✧ pastors/spiritual leaders

✧ missionaries

✧ employers, teachers, coaches, etc.

✧ governmental leaders

"Surely your goodness and love will follow me all the days of my life, and I will dwell in the house of the Lord forever."

✧ I thank You, God, for Your commitment to me.

✧ I thank You for the promise of eternal life.

✧ I praise You, God, for You are good, and Your mercies are new every morning. You are the best! There is none like You!

✧ I pray now, for those in my life who need to come to a decision to give their lives to Christ so that they may live in the house of the Lord forever. (List the names of those who need salvation.)

DAY 11

PRAYING THE NAMES OF GOD (PART 1)

Background: In the Old Testament, people gave descriptive names to who God was based on their experience. *Jehovah* is the basic Hebrew pronunciation for God. A descriptive term was added to that name as a descriptor. Also, the name of a person was descriptive of their character. So we are praying for the very real character of God to be manifested in our world.

God, You are *Jehovah-Shammah* (the Lord Who is always present with me).

✧ I thank You for Your presence. I invite You to be present in my life.

✧ May my family be flooded today with an awareness of Your presence.

You are *Jehovah-Jireh* (the Lord Who is my provision and meets all my needs).

✧ Thank You for the many ways You have provided for me. (List the things you are thankful for.)

✧ I pray for specific needs that I have today, because I believe You are my provider. (List specific things you need God to provide.)

You are *Jehovah-Rapha* (the Lord Who is my healer).

✧ Thank You, God, for my health.

✧ I pray for people who need healing. (List specific people who need healing.)

You are *Jehovah-Shalom* (the Lord Who is my peace and Who makes my life complete).

✧ Thank You for Your promised desire to make my life overflow with Your abundance (John 10:10).

✦ I trust You today with all of my life, and I receive Your peace.

✦ I declare *shalom* (completeness and peace) for myself, my family, and over my personal sphere of influence.

You are *Jehovah-Tsidekenu* (the Lord Who is my righteousness).

✦ God, I thank You for the finished work of Christ on the cross and that You have completely forgiven my sins.

✦ God, I ask you to reveal any area of unrighteousness— anything that is not right in my life. Please forgive me and transform me.

✦ I receive Your forgiveness, and I forgive myself. I choose to walk in Your righteousness. Thank You, God, that I am completely clean and forgiven because of the blood covering of Jesus.

You are *Jehovah-Rohi* (the Lord my Shepherd) and *Jehovah-Tsuri* (the Lord my Rock).

✦ Today, I choose to rest in Your care and to find security and strength in Your presence. You are my Shepherd who leads and guides me. You are my Rock, my stability, and the foundation upon which I stand.

✦ I place my life under Your authority, and I surrender my life to Your leadership. I declare that not my will but Yours be done in my life.

✦ I choose to be still and know that you are God (see Psalm 46:10).

✦ Read aloud a psalm of security such as 23, 46, 91, or 62.

You are *Jehovah-Nissi* (the Lord Who fights for me; my warrior, Who brings victory when I lift up the banner of His name).

✦ God, You have given me victory over every spiritual attack.

✧ I pray Your hedge of protection around me and my family today.

✧ I ask You, God, for victory in (name a specific battle you are facing today).

✧ I ask You to fight on my behalf and to be my defender.

✧ As Moses did when the Israelites were fighting the Amalekites, I lift my hands to the Lord and declare that I trust You today (Exodus 17).

You are Jesus!

As Isaiah declared (9:6–7), You are Wonderful Counselor, Mighty God, Everlasting Father, Prince of Peace. You are coming back and will reign on the throne of David. I declare Your ultimate authority over this universe (and of the increase of Your rulership and power there will be no end).

I declare You as my Savior and the Master of my life!

DAY 12

PRAYING BREAKTHROUGH PRAYERS (PART 1)

Background: We can often be held back by what the Bible regards as "strongholds" (a wrong pattern of thinking, desiring, or choosing). Spiritual strongholds must be broken so they can no longer hold us back. As we break them, we step into new areas of freedom in our lives.

Confessions of Praise: Based on Ephesians 2:1–10

- ✧ I praise You, Jesus, that You have overcome the Devil and the darkness through the cross. You hold the keys to death. Jesus, You sit at the right hand of the Father, not just as the Son of God, but as the Son of Man.

- ✧ I thank You for inviting me to be seated with You (Ephesians 2:1–6) in the heavenly realms. I now have every right to overcome the darkness. I have authority in Your name.

- ✧ Thank You for saving me from the wages of sin which is death.

- ✧ Thank You for filling me with the Holy Spirit. You are the power that fills my life.

- ✧ Thank You for rescuing me from the domination of the prince of the power of the air (the Devil). You have freed me from living a life of gratifying the desires of my sinful nature. Thank You that I am no longer an object destined for destruction because You have set me free to serve You for eternity.

- ✧ Help me to know the hope to which I have been called, the riches of my inheritance as a child of God, and the surpassing great power that can be released in my life as I believe in You (Ephesians 1).

Breakthrough #1: Overcoming Sexual Sin

✧ Lord, forgive me for any compromise in this area.

✧ I choose to allow You to purify my thoughts, my relationships, my desires, and my body.

✧ I confess that You forgive my sin completely and that I'm not dirty or stained in any way. I'm free by the blood of the cross.

✧ I break any soul-ties with unrighteous relationships of the past, and I ask You to take back any ground that I may have yielded to the Enemy.

(Note: If there is a recurring pattern of failure in this area, you need to confess to a spiritual leader or trusted friend. See James 5:16.)

Breakthrough #2: Overcoming Self-Gratification

✧ Lord, I choose not to medicate my pain with any substances (food, drugs, alcohol, etc.), but rather I depend upon the fullness of the Holy Spirit today.

✧ I'm willing to accept the temporary trials of life in order to gain the development of my character (Romans 8:28–29).

✧ I declare that God's grace is sufficient for me in every way, and that I am complete in Him. I choose to live in joy.

Breakthrough #3: Overcoming the Curse

✧ I declare the promise of Genesis 12—that covenant children of God (descendants of Abraham's faith) will be blessed.

✧ I declare the promise that those who bless me will be blessed and that those who curse me will be cursed. I pray that all of the nations on earth will be blessed through my life and my family.

✧ I declare God's full promise and purpose to be fulfilled in my life, my family, and all those under my care. I'm breaking the chain of sin and destruction from generations past, and I am launching a new generation of blessing from this moment forward.

✧ I declare that I'm God's workmanship, His masterpiece in the making (Ephesians 2:10), and created in Christ Jesus for good works that He has prepared for me. I declare that this is my destiny.

✧ I declare that I'm a new creature in Christ (2 Corinthians 5:17), the old has gone, it is completely forgiven, and a new day has come. God sees me through the lens of a fresh start.

✧ I declare that God has the final word in my life. I will not be limited by the words of rejection from others or the lies that I have believed about myself in the past. I'm not limited by my past failures or the opinions of others. I can do all things through Christ who gives me strength (Philippians 4:13).

Breakthrough #4: Walking in the Spirit

✧ Holy Spirit, I recognize that I need You today. Would You be my constant companion throughout this day— my helper and my counselor? Lead me into all truth. I make myself available to be used by You. Speak to me. Reveal to me the needs You want me to meet and the words You want me to speak. I surrender my life to Your purpose. Have Your way in me.

DAY 13

PRAYING THE PRAYERS OF PAUL

Background: Paul prayed for people in the New Testament. He provides for us some powerful prayers that we can agree with, and since they are in the Bible, we know these prayers are agreeing with God's will.

Praise: Begin your worship time with a song
Declare what God has done:

◇ Jesus, You have paid for my sins!

◇ You have conquered all disease, death, and the Devil himself.

◇ You rose from the grave on the third day. You ascended into heaven.

◇ Today, You reign in the heavenly realms, and everything is placed under Your feet.

◇ You are committed to me and to my success. If You are for me, who can be against me?

◇ I declare You as the Lord of my life!

Preparation: Read Ephesians 6:11–19 and put on the armor of God.

◇ I put on the *helmet of salvation* and ask You to guard my mind with Your truth.

◇ I put on the *breastplate of righteousness* and thank You that I am forgiven through Christ. I ask You to purify my affections and appetites and make me long for the right things.

◇ I put on the *belt of truth* and thank You for a clear conscience (where there is sin you should confess it and ask His forgiveness).

✧ I place the *shoes of readiness* on my feet and make myself available to go where You want me to go and to do what You prompt me to do.

✧ I take up the *shield of faith* to reject every lie and temptation of the Devil.

✧ I raise up the *sword of the Spirit*, the Word of God, and I recognize Your Word as the basis for what I believe and what will come out of my mouth today.

✧ I invite the Holy Spirit to come into my life and fill me with His presence that I might bear much fruit.

Read Philippians 1:6–11 and declare the following:

✧ God, who began a good work in me, will carry it onto completion until the day of Christ Jesus (v. 6).

✧ I declare that my love (for God and for others) might abound more and more with knowledge and depth of insight.

✧ I declare that I may be able to approve what is best (and experience God's will in all my circumstances).

✧ I declare that I may be pure and blameless and understanding, so that I will one day stand faultless before God because of the cross.

✧ I declare that I would be filled with the fruit of righteousness and that my life might be aimed toward God's glory.

Read 1 Thessalonians 3:12–13 and declare the following:

✧ God, may You direct my way according to Your plan.

✧ I declare that the Lord would make me increase and abound in love for others and for all.

✧ I declare that God would strengthen my heart and establish me as holy and blameless in His sight.

Read Ephesians 3:16-19 and declare the following:

✧ I pray for (name a person) that out of Your glorious riches You would strengthen (name) with power through Your spirit in his/her inner being.

✧ And I pray that Christ may dwell in (name's) heart through faith.

✧ And I pray that (name) being rooted and grounded in love may have power to grasp how high, wide, deep, and long is the love of God in his/her life.

✧ And I pray that he/she may know this love that surpasses knowledge that he/she may be filled to the measure of all the fullness of God

Read Ephesians 3:20–21 and declare the following:

I worship You, O God, for You are able to do immeasurably more than all I can ask or even imagine, according to the power of the Holy Spirit that is at work within me.

I declare that You will receive glory in my life, my family, in Your church, and through the working of the risen Jesus Christ in this world. May He be glorified in us forever and ever, amen!

DAY 14

PRAYERS OF PRAISE

Background: Once a week, it's good to take a day just for worship. On these days, we purposefully reduce our requests, and we increase our focus on relationship with God and on replenishment.

Worship: Spend time declaring who God is. Consider using worship music. Maybe take a walk and enjoy God's creation. Don't rush through this season of worship. Decide to enjoy God's presence.

Sabbath Focus: Read and meditate on a passage of Scripture. Consider reading through one of the psalms or one of the stories of Jesus found in the gospels. Try the practice of journaling (see chapter 5 at the beginning of this book).

Declaration: Read aloud Psalm 62. Make it a personal declaration today.

Rest (practice Sabbath)**:**

- ✧ How will you cease from your normal work today?
- ✧ What activities would refresh you today?
- ✧ What can you do today that will truly replenish your body and soul?
- ✧ Think about ways to reduce the "noise" in your life.

Recalibrate: Take some time to get your life refocused.

- ✧ How are your daily habits? What needs to improve?
- ✧ Where is there compromise? What can you change?
- ✧ What false ideas are undermining your faith?
- ✧ Who do you need to forgive?
- ✧ To whom do you need to apologize?

Remember: Count your blessings.

- ✧ Make a list of the many ways that God has blessed you. You can make note of these in the space below.
- ✧ Consider what it means that Jesus died for you, that you are now saved from your sins, and that you have a relationship with the Almighty forever.

Praise: Close your time with God by again declaring His character and His goodness to you. Spend additional time in worship.

Use this space to list blessings and praises to God:

DAY 15

PRAYING GOD'S COVENANT BLESSINGS

Background: In Deuteronomy 28, Moses declared the blessings of God that would come to the people of Israel, who were in covenant relationship with God. These blessings represent for us what God wants for His people—His best and His will. So we pray for God's fullest blessing to be released upon us.

Praise: Begin by singing a song of worship; then declare the following:

✧ God, I praise You for Your good intentions toward me. You have said that You have plans to prosper me and not to harm me, to give me a future and a great hope (Jeremiah 29:11).

✧ God, I praise You for Your faithfulness to Your promises. You said that no matter how many promises You have made (2 Corinthians 1:20), they are yes in Christ. You have ratified every covenant promise by Christ's death on the cross. I say amen, so be it in my life.

✧ God, I praise You for Your redemptive capacity. You are able to work all things together for my good (Romans 8:28). You never waste my pain or trials, but You use them for my benefit.

Repentance: Read Deuteronomy 28:1–2 and declare the following:

✧ God, I thank You that I cannot earn Your blessings, but they are given as a gift through faith. I thank You that You have chosen to bless me.

✧ God, I also realize that I can undermine Your ability to bless me by walking in willful sin and disobedience.

Reveal to me any hindrances that keep me from Your blessings.

✧ I turn from (name specific sin) and choose to stop sinning. To the best of my ability, I pledge my obedience to You.

Declarations: Read Deuteronomy 28:3–14 and declare the following:

✧ I declare Your blessing on my location. Pour out Your favor and reveal Yourself to my home, neighborhood, workplace, and city (v. 3).

✧ I declare Your blessing on my ability to produce. Bless the work of my hands. Bless my children and prosper their efforts. Multiply the harvest of my life. Give me a multiplied return for all of my investments (v. 4).

✧ I declare Your blessing upon the intake of my life and of my family's life. May You protect us from any harm and any disease. May You keep us from any harmful intake of any media, any relationship, or any other source. May the diet of my life and the life of my home be free from destructive influences (v. 5).

✧ I declare Your blessing on my direction. May You go before me and prepare the way for my arrival with Your favor today (in appointments, meetings, etc). May You come behind me and favor the things left undone (v. 6).

✧ I declare Your victory over any spiritual attack against me, my home, and all those under my care. Though the Enemy comes at me in one direction, may he be so defeated that he will flee in seven directions (v. 7).

✧ I declare that You send a blessing on my finances and possessions, and everything that comes from the work of my hands. May You bless me and increase me in the destiny You have for me. Bless me to the degree that I also may overflow with resources for people in need and the advancement of Your kingdom (v. 8).

✧ I declare Your blessing on my spiritual life today. May You establish me as holy and special to You. May You give me a spiritual fullness so that I can walk in obedience to You and therefore in Your favor and in Your abiding presence (vv. 9–10).

✧ I declare Your abundant prosperity as Your will for my life. Breathe Your favor on my life (vv. 11–14).

✧ Send Your rain to refresh my life.

✧ Cause me to be the lender and not the borrower.

✧ Make me the head and not the tail, the top and not the bottom.

Reaffirmation: I choose to keep Your commandments and to live by Your ways. I will not turn to the right nor to the left. I will not worship anything other than You. God, You are the satisfaction of my life (v. 14).

DAY 16

PRAYING BREAKTHROUGH PRAYERS (PART 2)

Background: On day 12 of this prayer guide, we prayed through the first few areas of stronghold. Today, we will continue along those lines and declare freedom in Christ in every area of our lives.

Worship: Read aloud Colossians 1:15–20.

- ✧ I declare Jesus Christ as the One who has defeated the Devil and overcome death.
- ✧ Lord, I declare You as my Lord and as the ruler of the universe and of my life. I worship Jesus and none other.

Breakthrough #1: Overcoming Pride

- ✧ Lord, Your Word says that You oppose the proud but give grace to the humble (James 4:6). So I humble myself and declare my dependence on You in every way.
- ✧ Lord, You promise that if I humble myself before You, in due season You will lift me up. I appeal to You for that due season.

Breakthrough #2: Overcoming Demonic Attack

- ✧ Lord, Your Word says that I overcome the Devil by the blood of the Lamb (what You have already done on the cross) and by the word of my testimony (my confession of faith in You) (see Revelation 12:11).
- ✧ I renounce any curses or connections with the Enemy from the past, and I ask the Lord Jesus to take back any ground in my soul where I may have given the Devil a foothold (Ephesians 4:26–27).

- ✧ Therefore, I declare victory over every spiritual attack against my life, my family, and those under my care.
- ✧ I declare victory over every attack against my small group, my pastor, and my church family.
- ✧ I declare that Jesus' blood was shed for my loved ones who have not yet experienced salvation (list their names), and I claim victory over their soul(s) for Christ.

Breakthrough #3: Overcoming Bitterness

- ✧ Lord, I thank You for forgiving my sin completely. You have been so good and merciful to me.
- ✧ Because You have forgiven me unconditionally, I choose to forgive (list an offender) and release them from their offense toward me.
- ✧ I also choose to forgive myself for (list areas of guilt you may carry), and I release myself to experience the fullness of Your grace.
- ✧ I choose to trust You completely, and I release You to do whatever You feel is best in my life.

Breakthrough Requests:

- ✧ Pray for areas of financial breakthrough needed in your life and/or business.
- ✧ Pray for breakthrough miracles of healing or provision in your life and in people's lives.
- ✧ Pray for breakthrough miracles in the lives and relationships of those in your family.
- ✧ Pray for breakthrough for your local church and the needs you are aware of.
- ✧ Pray for breakthrough for missionaries and the needs of their work you are aware of.

Breakthrough Praise: Read 2 Chronicles 20 and declare the following:

- ✧ Lord, just as praise was a weapon in the days of Jehoshaphat, so I believe that as I worship You today,

You will send Your angelic host ahead of me to bring victory in every area of my life.

✧ I trust that You will make the valley of my trial to be transformed into the valley of praise (2 Chronicles 20:26).

✧ I declare victory so great in my life that You will take what the Devil meant for evil and turn it around for my good. I declare that the victory will be so great that I will not only be delivered from this attack, but that I will plunder the Enemy.

✧ Restore to me and to my family everything that the Enemy has tried to destroy. Do it all for Your glory.

DAY 17

PRAYING ROMANS 8

Background: Romans 8 is one of the great expressions of God's incredible love for us. It represents His will as granted to us by His gracious choice. As we pray these promises, we agree with God's choice to bless us.

Read Romans 8

Praise:

✧ Thank You that there is now no condemnation for me because I am in Christ Jesus! And that the law of the Spirit of life has set me free from the law of sin and death (vv. 1–2).

✧ Thank You for adopting me into Your family and making me Your child. Thank You that I can relate to You as my Father (Abba—Daddy God) (vv. 15–16).

✧ Thank You that not only have You made me Your child, but You have made me an heir of the kingdom and a coheir with Christ. All of the resources of the kingdom are available to me through Christ. The riches of heaven have been willed to me (v. 17).

✧ I now pray from that position. I'm an heir with Christ. I have authority in the kingdom. I'm not a beggar. I'm a member of God's royal family. I'm a rightful owner of God's promises. I outrank the demons of hell, and they must listen to my commands. I humbly receive my rights as a child of God.

Confession:

✧ I confess that I cannot become righteous through determination to keep the rules. It is only Your Spirit living in me that gives me the hope of a holy life (vv. 3–4).

✧ Forgive me for the times in this past week when I chose to do what my sinful nature desired. Reveal to me where my sinful nature is directing or dominating my life (vv. 5–8).

✧ Holy Spirit, I desire close fellowship with You today. Help me to be aware of Your promptings and to rely on You to birth obedience in me. I choose to obey You and to seek to please the Spirit today (vv. 9–11).

✧ I choose to put to death the misdeeds of my body, my mind, my lips, and my attitudes. I choose to live up to who I am in Christ (a child of God) (vv. 12–15).

Prayer for Redemption: Read Romans 8:18–27 and declare the following:

✧ Lord, I recognize that the emptiness inside me and the longings within me are really longings for You and for heaven. Satisfy me with Your presence today.

✧ God, I pray for my loved ones who don't know you (name them). They also are longing for satisfaction and running after it in so many ways. Help them to see that what they really long for Is You. Draw them to Yourself today.

✧ God, the earth itself is convulsing under the curse of sin and the domination of the Devil and evil power. May You redeem this world. May Your kingdom come today in my family, in my church, in my neighborhood, in my city, in my workplace, and in this nation.

✧ Holy Spirit, I recognize that You groan within me to see situations in my life and people around me redeemed. I release You to work through me today. Use me to release Your purpose and promises in the world today.

Declarations of Triumph:

✧ Thank You for working on my behalf in all things and using even my trials and painful moments for Your purpose. Thank You for Your commitment to my character to make me like Christ. I surrender my life situations to You today and trust You to work them for my benefit. I trust You in all things today (vv. 28–29).

✧ I declare that I am more than a conqueror today. I will not just survive my life today—I will overcome and conquer (v. 37).

✧ I pray for the people in my life. I ask You to make them more than conquerors in what they are facing today. (Pray specifically for individuals by name.)

✧ I pray for pastors and missionaries today (by name). Make them to be more than conquerors in what they are facing today.

Declarations of Praise:

✧ Thank You that You are for me and not against me and that You are willing to give me ALL things— whatever I need (vv. 31–32).

✧ Thank You that You will never stop loving me (read the verses aloud, 35–39).

✧ Thank you that you accept me in Christ, no matter what, and that Your decision to love and accept me is a choice You have made that I can't diminish. You have chosen to love me and there is nothing I can do to increase that and nothing I can do to make You stop.

✧ Lord, may the people under my care recognize these truths today. May they feel Your unconditional, unfailing love in their lives today. In Jesus name, Amen!

DAY 18

PRAYING SCRIPTURE PRAYERS

Background: Paul prayed for the people in the churches he planted. These prayers we can pray with great confidence as they are inspired by the Holy Spirit and recorded for us in the Bible.

Praise: Read aloud Romans 11:33–36

Pray Colossians 1:9–14

- ✧ May God fill me and those in my family with the knowledge of His will through all the wisdom and understanding that the Spirit gives.

- ✧ May God equip us to live a life worthy of the Lord and to please Him in every way.

- ✧ May God cause us to bear fruit in every good work, and to grow in the knowledge of God, being strengthened with all power according to His glorious might, so that we might have great endurance, patience, and joy regardless of the circumstances.

- ✧ We thank You, God, that You have qualified us to share in the inheritance of Your holy people and that You have rescued us from the dominion of darkness and brought the kingdom of light, the kingdom of the Son, whom You love.

- ✧ Thank You God, that we are redeemed and forgiven of all our sins in You alone.

Pray 1 Thessalonians 5:22–23

- ✧ May God Himself, the God of peace, sanctify me (purify and make right in every area of my life), through and through.

✧ May my whole spirit, soul, and body be kept blameless and healthy until the coming of Jesus.

✧ May God, who has called me, and is faithful, fulfill His will for my life.

Pray 3 John 2

✧ I pray that (names) would prosper in every way and be in health. I ask that they would live out of a healthy and abundant soul and that God's best would explode from within into every area of their world.

Pray Ephesians 1:17–21

✧ May God, give (names) the Spirit of wisdom and revelation so that they may know Jesus better.

✧ I pray that the eyes of their hearts may be enlightened in order that they may know the hope to which they have been called, the riches of their glorious inheritance (as a part of God's people), and the incomparably great power that can be released into their world as they believe.

✧ I pray that (names) may walk in the power of God— the same power that was exerted when God raised Christ from the dead and seated Jesus at the right hand of the Father.

✧ May you resurrect the dead areas in (names') lives. May you cause them to understand their destiny and the authority that they have in Jesus.

Pray 2 Thessalonians 3:1–5, 16

✧ I pray that You would cause the message of Jesus to spread rapidly in my family, in my city, and in this world—that Jesus would be honored in every way.

✧ I pray that (name) would be delivered from wicked and evil influences, for not everyone is a person of faith.

✧ I declare that the Lord is faithful and that He will strengthen and protect (name) from the Evil One.

✧ May the Lord direct (name's) heart into the love of God and into the steadfastness that comes from connectedness to Christ.

✧ May the God of peace, Himself, give (name) peace at all times and in every way. May the Lord be with that person.

Pray Hebrews 13:20

✧ May the God of peace, who through the blood of the eternal covenant brought our Lord Jesus back from the dead, that great Shepherd of the sheep, may He equip (name) with every good thing for doing His will.

✧ May He work in us what is pleasing to Him through Jesus Christ, to whom belongs glory forever and ever, amen!

Declare Jude 24–25

✧ Now, to Him who is able to keep us from falling and present us before His glorious presence without fault and with great joy, to the only God, our Savior, be glory, majesty, power, and authority, through Jesus Christ, our Lord, before all ages, now and forevermore, amen!

DAY 19

PRAYING PSALM 16

Background: The psalms were all songs written out of pain or personal struggle. They are great expressions of honesty and trust. As we pray them, we are praying according to words that were inspired by the Holy Spirit out of pain.

Declaration of Trust: *"Keep me safe, my God, for in you I take refuge. I say to the LORD, 'You are my Lord; apart from you I have no good thing'"* (vv. 1–2).

- ✧ I declare that You are my fortress, my place of safety. My heart is secure in Your care.
- ✧ You are the Lord (the I AM). You are dependent on nothing. You are completely sufficient in every way.
- ✧ You are my Lord. I thank You that You are committed to my well-being. You own me as a father owns his child.
- ✧ You are the sole source of all good things in my life. I will look to You and You only as the fount of my satisfaction.

Prayer of Commitment: *"I say of the holy people who are in the land, 'They are the noble ones in whom is all my delight'"* (v 3).

- ✧ I recognize that I belong to You and to Your family, O God. You are my Abba Father (Daddy).
- ✧ I commit myself to the members of my small group and local church. Bless Your family, O God.
- ✧ I pray for the needs of people in my church family (be specific), my pastors, and any missionaries (list some by name).

Prayer of Repentance: *"Those who run after other gods will suffer more and more. I will not pour out their libations of blood to such gods or take up their names on my lips"* (v. 4).

✧ Forgive me, God, for running to anything other than You to find rest in my times of stress.

✧ Forgive me for trying to medicate my pain through (name anything you have used). I now turn my hurts over to You and ask You to heal my heart.

✧ And I choose to forgive (name a person), and I release them from their offenses toward me, in Jesus name.

✧ I place you, Jesus, on the throne of my life.

Prayer for Increase: *"Lord, you alone are my portion and my cup; you make my lot secure. The boundary lines have fallen for me in pleasant places; surely I have a delightful inheritance"* (vv. 5–6).

✧ God, I thank You for the many ways You have blessed me. (List some things you are thankful for)

✧ I ask You now to enlarge my territory and expand my influence.

✧ Place Your hedge of protection around my family and all that is under my care.

✧ I pray also for You to bless (name specific people in your life who you want to see grow in Christ).

✧ I pray that God will give me an inheritance of souls. (Pray specifically for people who need Christ.)

Time to Hear: *"I will praise the Lord, who counsels me; even at night my heart instructs me"* (v. 7).

✧ Spend a few minutes in worship or in Bible meditation. (Pick a verse to think deeply about, or consider journaling about that verse).

✧ Listen to the promptings of the Holy Spirit. (Consider writing those thoughts down somewhere as well.)

Prayer Declarations: Pray these verses for yourself, or pray them for a loved one or family member (insert their name as you pray).

✧ I have set the Lord always before me. Because He is at my right hand, I will not be shaken (v. 8).

✧ Therefore my heart is glad and my tongue rejoices; my body also will rest secure (v. 9).

✧ Because You will not abandon me to the grave, nor will You let your faithful one see decay (v. 10).

✧ You have made known to me the path of life; You will fill me with joy in Your presence, with eternal pleasures at Your right hand (v. 11).

Praise Time: I thank You, God, for Your eternal nature. You are the first and the last, the Alpha and Omega, the beginning and the end. You are holy, holy, holy. You are the One who was, and is, and is to come!

DAY 20

PRAYING THE BEATITUDES

Background: We have record of Jesus' most famous message found in Matthew 5, commonly known as the Sermon on the Mount. He began this message by listing eight qualities that God blesses. These eight qualities are favored by God and are therefore His will.

Be-attitude #1: God approves of me (and blesses me) when I am poor and not when I am perfect.

- ✧ God, Your approval is not based on my success but rather on my humble dependence upon You in every way. Without You, I am nothing and I can do nothing. But with You, anything is possible (v. 3).
- ✧ God, help me in the areas where I feel weak and helpless.
- ✧ I declare that Your grace is sufficient and that I will overcome as I place my trust in You.

Be-attitude #2: God approves of me when I share His sorrow.

- ✧ God, breathe Your favor upon me as I mourn over the things that break Your heart.
- ✧ I grieve over my sin and over the brokenness of people who are hurting and those who are lost (v. 4).
- ✧ Thank You for Your forgiveness of my sin.
- ✧ God, reveal to me people's needs that burden Your heart today.

Be-attitude #3: God approves of me when I yield my rights to Him and let Him fight for me.

- ✧ When I yield my rights to You, You move all of heaven

and earth for me. (This is yielding of rights, not the yielding of responsibilities.)

✧ God, empower me to fulfill my responsibilities by Your grace. I choose to yield my rights to You (v. 5).

✧ I yield my right to be appreciated, understood, valued, and (you fill in the blank with whatever other rights have recently been violated).

✧ I also yield my right to decide what happens with my money, my possessions, my body, my mind, my future, my relationships, my life, and my ministry.

✧ God, as I surrender to You, I ask You to move in my specific situations of need.

Be-attitude #4: God approves of me when I hunger and thirst to be like Jesus.

✧ God, thank You for Your great favor when I choose to align myself with Your character.

✧ I long to be like Jesus more than I long for my own way, my own ease, my own comfort, or my own pleasure. May I sense Your approval today (v. 6).

Be-attitude #5: God approves of me when I am pure in heart.

✧ God, I purposefully lay aside pride, self-centeredness, and personal gain to please You.

✧ I open my heart to see more of You.

✧ Grant me a greater revelation of who You are (v. 7).

✧ God, purify my heart. I repent of self-centeredness and pride.

✧ I pray David's prayer: *"May these words of my mouth and this meditation of my heart be pleasing in your sight, Lord, my Rock and my Redeemer"* (Psalm 19:14).

Be-attitude #6: God approves of me when I am merciful.

✧ God, I choose mercy, and I desire to remain in the flow of Your mercy in my own life.

✧ May I not become bitter, vindictive, or slanderous so that Your mercy will flow in my life.

✧ Your Word says, "Mercy triumphs over judgment" (James 2:13). As I choose mercy, may Your mercy and grace be evident in my own life.

✧ I choose to forgive (name anyone who has offended you), and I release them from this offense.

✧ God, I ask you to heal my heart and cause me to triumph over this situation.

Be-attitude #7: God approves of me when I am a peacemaker.

✧ You are a Father who desires harmony to dwell in Your family. May I protect the family of God by sowing peace (v. 9).

✧ God, may I sow peace and not division so that I will be pleasing in Your sight. "Peacemakers who sow in peace reap a harvest of righteousness" (James 3:18).

✧ I pray for peace in my family, my workplace, my small group, and in my church.

✧ Forgive me for any bad attitudes, gossip, or slander.

Be-attitude #8: God approves of me when I rejoice in persecution, false accusation, trials, and attack.

✧ I pray that Your favor will rest upon me as I walk in faith, and help me to not seek immediate gratification (vv. 11–12).

✧ God, I choose to rejoice in my suffering. May I value Your long-term and eternal rewards more than I value temporary and passing immediate rewards.

✧ I thank You, God, for my eternal reward.

✧ Thank You that You never waste my pain but use it for Your eternal purposes (Romans 8:28–29).

✧ Teach me to number my days wisely and to live today in light of eternity (Psalm 90:12).

DAY 21

PRAYING PSALM 19—A DAY OF PRAISE

Background: Psalm 19 talks about God as a creator. As we take today to worship, we will use this psalm to help us recognize who God is.

Worship: Begin your season of prayer with a time of worship. Use some worship music or get alone and sing to God.

Declare God Through His Creation.
- ✧ Read aloud Psalm 19:1–6.
- ✧ Meditate on the wonder of God's creative works in the world.
- ✧ Consider taking a walk outdoors. Notice the little evidences of God's design.
- ✧ List the ways that creation reveals God's power and genius.

Declare God Through His Word.
- ✧ Read aloud Psalm 19:7–11.
- ✧ Thank God for the consistency and dependability of His promises.
- ✧ Meditate on some of your favorite biblical promises. Think on the meaning of every word. Thank God for the promises that specifically apply in your life.

Declare God Through His Holiness.
- ✧ Read aloud Psalm 19:12–13.
- ✧ Thank God that He is not evil in any way and will never sin or do harm. Praise Him that He never changes and does not fail.

✧ Meditate on what it means that God is holy, holy, holy. (The word *holy* means: special or distinct, set apart, without evil, pure.)

Prayer:

✧ Read aloud Psalm 19:14.

✧ Consider the words you have been speaking: Do they align with God? Are they of faith? Is there blessing or cursing? Are you negative or critical? Do you sound like God or like the Devil?

✧ Consider the meditations of your heart: Are you thinking right? Is there lust? Is there grumbling? Do you imagine the worst or the best?

✧ Ask for God to purify your heart and your speech.

Use this space to list blessings and praises to God:

DAY 22

PRAYING PSALM 20

Background: Psalm 20 is a prayer that asks for God's best. It could be called a psalm of blessing—a psalm we can use to speak life and faith over someone else.

Praise: *"May the Lord answer you when you are in distress; may the name of the God of Jacob protect you. May he send you help from the sanctuary and grant you support from Zion"* (vv. 1–2).

- ✧ God I thank You that You answer me when I am in distress. You care about my life's issues.
- ✧ May Your Name protect me. Your Name represents Your character. (Praise God for His many wonderful qualities.)
- ✧ May You send me help from the sanctuary (the place of praise) and grant me help from Zion (the place of Your presence). I declare that this season of worship will bring me the help and support I need.

Confession: *"May He remember all your sacrifices and accept your burnt offerings"* (v. 3).

- ✧ Jesus, I thank You that Your sacrifice on the cross was enough to provide for my cleansing and restoration.
- ✧ I now offer my life to You as a living sacrifice in response to what You have done for me.
- ✧ I turn from specific sins (thoughts, words, attitudes, actions).
- ✧ Thank You, Jesus, that You were willing to pay the ultimate price for my forgiveness. I am so grateful.

Requests: *"May He give you the desire of your heart and make all your plans succeed"* (v 4).

- ✧ Pray for your heart's desires. (List them specifically.)
- ✧ Pray for today's plans. Commit them to God's care. (List them.)
- ✧ Pray for your family's needs and desires. (List them.)
- ✧ Ask God to bless those you know who have needs (pray specifically).

Advanced Thanksgiving: *"May we shout for joy over your victory and lift up our banners in the name of our God. May the Lord grant all your requests. Now this I know: The Lord gives victory to his anointed. He answers him from his heavenly sactuary with the victorious power of his right hand"* (vv. 5–6).

- ✧ I declare that God will bring victory in every area of my life. Jesus has conquered sin, death, the Devil, and every disease. I declare that I am more than a conqueror because He has loved me and chosen me.
- ✧ I raise the banner of the Lord (like a battalion raises its flag). He is Jehovah-Nissi—the God who fights for me. He is a Warrior. He is backing me.
- ✧ I declare that God's mighty hand is able to do all things. He hears me when I pray. He answers prayer.
- ✧ I declare His will be done in all of my requests. I declare His kingdom come in every situation and relationship of my life.

Declaration of Trust: *"Some trust in chariots and some in horses, but we trust in the name of the Lord our God. They are brought to their knees and fall, but we rise up and stand firm"* (vv. 7–8).

- ✧ I choose today to no longer depend on (name what you are tempted to trust in other than God). I trust in the name of (character of) my God.
- ✧ I choose to trust God with (list your burdens). God, I give You my problems, and in exchange, I receive Your peace.

- ✧ You will cause me to rise up and stand firm. I will not be shaken. I will rest secure in Your care.

PRAISE/PRAY: *"Lord, give victory to the king! Answer us when we call"* (v. 9)!

- ✧ I praise You, God, that You have heard and answered me.
- ✧ I pray for those in authority in my life (president, boss, teachers, coaches, pastors).
- ✧ I thank You, God, that You are my ultimate authority and that my life is completely under Your care. In Jesus' name, amen!

DAY 23

PRAYING THE NAMES OF GOD (PART 2)

Background: On Day 11 of this prayer guide, we prayed through some of the Hebrew names for God. (You can refer back to that section for more information.) Each of His names represents an aspect of His character we can know by experience.

You are *El Shaddai* (the God who is sufficient for all things; who has made covenant with me).

⬦ Lord, You are almighty. There is nothing that is too difficult for You.

⬦ Lord, You are all sufficient. All that I need is found in You. You are overflowing with goodness and grace.

⬦ Lord, You are a covenant-keeper. What You have promised, You will fulfill. I choose to trust You.

You are *El Kanna* (the God who is jealous for me) and *Esh Oklah* (the God who is a consuming fire).

⬦ God, I thank You that You are passionate about Your relationship with me. Thank You that You love me so much that You are jealous of anything that would take me away from You and of anything that might be destructive to my life.

⬦ I choose You above all things. Forgive me for anything that I have worshipped by believing it would be a source of satisfaction for me.

⬦ Forgive me for running to things other than to You when I am discouraged.

⬦ Burn away the things in my life that are sinful or destructive. Help me not to cause Your Spirit to grieve.

You are *Jehovah-Tsebaoth* (the Lord of Hosts).

✧ I recognize that You rule over everything and that the angels and demons submit to Your name.

✧ Break the power of the Enemy over my life, my family, my small group, church, and my community.

✧ Release Your angels to form a hedge of protection around my life, my family, and all that is under my care.

✧ I join You in my prayer and agree for the hosts of heaven to defeat the powers of darkness today.

You are *Abba* (Daddy God).

✧ I recognize You as my loving heavenly Father. Thank You for choosing me. Thank You for adopting me into Your family. Thank You for the wonderful and eternal inheritance that I have in Christ.

✧ I thank You, God, for the specific ways that You, as my Father, have provided for me in the past. (Mention some specific instances.)

✧ I ask You to meet these specific needs for me (name your needs).

You are *Baal-Perizim* (the God of great breakthrough— 2 Samuel 5).

✧ Lord, just as You went ahead of David and brought breakthrough victory on his behalf, may You go ahead of me today. Just as the waters break out from a bursting dam, may You break out before me.

✧ I pray for breakthrough miracles in these areas of my life (be specific about finances, areas of healing, or salvations).

You are *El-Elyon* (the Highest God).

✧ Read Isaiah 40. Read some portions aloud to God.

✧ God, I recognize You as the ruler over all things and the ruler over my life. I humble myself in Your sight.

As the Bible promises, in due time, You will lift me up. I trust You with my future.

✧ Lord, You rule over the world. I pray Your kingdom to come and will to be done in the governments of this world:

✧ Pray for governmental leaders.

✧ Pray for church leaders.

✧ Pray for employers and business leaders.

You are *El-Roi* (the God who sees me).

✧ Read Psalm 121 with a spirit of praise.

✧ Lord, I invite You into my day. Help me to be conscious of Your presence all day long. Make me aware of Your voice in my life. Speak to me.

✧ I choose to enjoy You and to worship You today.

DAY 24

PRAYING PSALM 46

Background: Psalm 46 was prayed in times of great instability. It expresses God's will for us to find our strength in God.

Declaration of Praise: *"God is our refuge and strength, an ever-present help in trouble"* (v 1).

- ✧ Thank You, God, that You are a place of security and safety. You are a fortress, a refuge, a hiding place, and a strong tower. When I run into You, I am safe.
- ✧ You are my strength. You sustain my soul. Your grace is totally sufficient.
- ✧ You are ever present, especially in times of trouble. You will never leave me and never forsake me.
- ✧ You are all powerful, all knowing, always present, unchanging, faithful, and true. You are trustworthy.

Declaration of Trust: *"Therefore we will not fear, though the earth give way and the mountains fall into the heart of the sea, though its waters roar and foam and the mountains quake with their surging"* (vv. 2–3).

- ✧ I choose today to trust God. His care in my life is more stable than anything on earth.
- ✧ I choose faith over fear. I refuse to imagine the worst. Instead, I will imagine the wonderful deliverance and future God has in store for me.
- ✧ I trust God with (name the problems and challenges), and I place these situations in His hands.

Declaration of Relationship: *"There is a river [the Holy Spirit] whose streams make glad the city of [person belonging to] God, [my heart is] the holy place where the Most High dwells. God is* *within [me], [I] will not fall; God will help [me] at break of day"* (vv. 4–5).

✧ Holy Spirit, I invite you into my day. Speak to me. Lead me. Fill me with Your presence. I depend on You.

✧ Holy Spirit, draw my loved ones to Jesus. (Pray for those who need Christ by name. Ask the Spirit of God to bring conviction into their lives and to open their eyes to Jesus.)

Prayer for Family: *"Nations are in uproar, kingdoms fall; he lifts his voice, the earth melts. The Lord Almighty is with us; the God of Jacob is our fortress"* (vv. 6–7).

✧ I now pray a hedge of God's protection around my life and all those under my care.

✧ I pray for God's almighty power to be released on behalf of (name specific people and pray for specific needs).

✧ I declare God's covenant promises over my family, my church, and my small group. Just as God was committed to Jacob (Israel), so I know He is now in covenant with me.

✧ I pray for God's wisdom, grace, and provision to be given to the leaders in my nation. (Pray for them by name and for specific things of need.)

Declaration of Victory: *"Come and see what the Lord has done, the desolations he has brought on the earth. He makes wars cease to the ends of the earth. He breaks the bow and shatters the spear; he burns the shields with fire. He says, 'Be still and know that I am God'"* (vv. 8–10).

✧ Thank You, Jesus, that You have defeated the Devil and every enemy against me by Your death, burial, and resurrection.

✧ I declare victory over sickness, sin, and Satan.

✧ I choose to cease striving and rest in the victory You have already provided to my life.

✧ I say to my soul "be still," and I declare that You are God. You will take care of what concerns me.

Declaration of Praise: "'Be still [cease striving, stop worrying] and know that I am God; I will be exalted among the nations [people in your life], I will be exalted in the earth [the place where you live].' The Lord Almighty is with us [me]; the God of Jacob is our [my] fortress" (vv. 10–11).

DAY 25

PRAYING THE FRUITS OF THE SPIRIT

Background: Galatians 5:22–23 records for us the qualities that the Holy Spirit births in us when we are relationship with Him. It is easy to see how these nine qualities are God's will for us.

Focus 1: Lord, birth goodness in me today.

✧ Begin by praising God for His goodness. How is He good in His nature? How has He been good to you?

✧ Pray Romans 8:28–29. Lord, You promised that You would work everything together for my good. Use the difficulties of my life to make me like You.

Focus 2: Lord, birth faithfulness in me today.

✧ Read John 15:1–9. Today, I choose to connect into the vine of Jesus Christ, and I ask that the life of God would flow in me, produce much fruit, and that I might glorify God.

✧ Forgive me for any areas of disobedience and unfaithfulness (confess specific sins).

✧ Reveal anything to me, O Lord, that might hinder my connectedness to You. Fill me with Your Spirit.

Focus 3: Lord, birth love in my life today.

✧ I pray for my family today that they may have the strength to comprehend what is the breadth, and the length, and the height, and the depth and to know the love of Christ that surpasses knowledge, that they may be filled with all the fullness of God (see Ephesians 3:18–19).

✧ Lord, I thank You that You love me unconditionally and that You accept me because of Christ. There is nothing I can do to increase it, and there is nothing I can do to diminish it (see Romans 8:31–39).

Focus 4: Lord, birth infectious joy in my life today.

✧ I choose joy, even in trials, because You are using these things to make me mature, complete, and lacking nothing.

✧ I declare that the joy of the Lord is my strength (my fortress and protective hedge—see Nehemiah 8:10). May the joy of the Lord be a hedge for all those under my care.

Focus 5: Lord, birth peace in my life today.

✧ I trust You, Lord, with the following situations that cause me stress/anxiety (list them). I declare that You are good and will do what is best for me. May the peace of God, which is beyond understanding, guard my heart and mind in Christ Jesus (see Philippians 4:6–7).

✧ Father, may Your peace rest on those who are struggling (name specific individuals).

Focus 6: Lord, birth patience in my life today.

✧ Read Psalm 40 aloud.

✧ As Jesus prayed, I pray now: "not my will but Yours be done."

Focus 7: Lord, birth kindness in my life today.

✧ Forgive me Lord, for any words, attitudes, or actions that have been unkind. Help me make things right and make restitution for what I have done.

✧ Lord, open my eyes to the person You want me to love and serve who is hurting or in need today.

Focus 8: Lord, birth self-control in my life today.

✧ I declare that You are able to set me free from the habits of the past. I renounce and put to death the old ways and choose to live for You.

✧ I choose to live to please God today. As I obey the moment-by-moment promptings of the Spirit, I will not just survive—I will overcome.

Focus 9: Lord, birth meekness and gentleness in my life.

✧ I declare Your promise that as I yield my rights to You, You will move heaven and earth on my behalf (Matthew 5:8).

✧ I yield control to You over all my life. (Ask God for the specific ways that you need Him to provide today.)

✧ I declare Your ability and power in my life. As I delight myself in You, grant me the desires of my heart (Psalm 37:4–5).

DAY 26

PRAYING PSALM 91

Background: Psalm 91 is a declaration of trust in God despite circumstances of extreme stress and pressure. This passage is a great one to pray when there is a lot of turbulence and trouble in your life.

Praise: *"Whoever dwells in the shelter of the Most High will rest in the shadow of the Almighty"* (v. 1).

- ✧ I praise You for who You are — the Almighty, the Most High (above all).
- ✧ *"I will say of the Lord, 'He is my refuge and my fortress, my God, in whom I trust'"* (v. 2).
- ✧ *"Surely He will save [me] from the fowler's snare [who sets traps] and from the deadly pestilence"* (v. 3).
- ✧ *"He will cover [me] with his feathers, and under his wings [I] will find refuge [like a baby bird cared for in a storm by his mother]; his faithfulness will be [my] shield and rampart"* (v. 4).

Declarations of Trust:

- ✧ *"[I] will not fear the terror of night, nor the arrow that flies by day, nor the pestilence that stalks in the darkness, nor the plague that destroys at midday"* (vv. 5–6).
- ✧ *"A thousand may fall at [my] side, ten thousand at [my] right hand, but it will not come near [me, my family, or those under my care]"* (v. 7).
- ✧ *"[I] will only observe with [my] eyes and see the punishment of the wicked"* (v. 8).

✧ As I make the Most High my dwelling—even the Lord, who is my refuge, then no harm will befall me, no disaster will come near my household (see vv. 9–10).

Request:

✧ God, would You command Your angels concerning my family (spouse, kids, parents)? Send angels to protect and preserve them in all their ways (v. 11).

✧ I ask You to lift my life and my family up in Your hands. Bless our coming and going. Bless the work of our hands. Keep us from harm (v. 12).

✧ Cause us to walk in victory over every evil attack. May we *"tread on the lion and the cobra"* (v. 13).

Confession: Consider where you are working against God in your life:

✧ Forgive me for _____ (words, attitudes, actions).

✧ I choose to forgive my offender (name), and I release that person from _____. Please heal my wounded heart.

✧ I will do what You are asking me to do. (Consider anything God has told you to do that you have not yet stepped out to do.)

Specific Prayer Needs:

✧ Pray for those who are sick

✧ Pray for those who are struggling

✧ Pray for pastors and missionaries

✧ Pray for soldiers serving in harm's way

✧ Pray for at least three friends who don't know Christ

✧ Pray for your president and government leaders

Thanksgiving: (vv. 14–16)

✧ Thank You, God, that You love me.

✧ Thank You that You have promised to protect me and rescue me because I acknowledge Your name.

- ✧ Thank You that when I call upon You, You do answer me. (Recount specific provisions and answers to prayer.) Thank You that You deliver me/honor me.
- ✧ Thank You that You are with me in trouble.
- ✧ Thank You for Your promise to satisfy me with long life. May it be. Give me health and life.
- ✧ Thank You that You have given me salvation. Thank You for the cross of Jesus that made a way for me.

Declaration of Trust: So I enter this day choosing to rest in You. You are my refuge. You are my place of safety. I trust in Your power and in Your care for my life.

I choose to abide under the shadow of the Almighty!

DAY 27

PRAYING OUT OF ACTS 2

Background: Acts chapter 2 is the record of the birth of the church. It is one of the greatest moments in human history and is a reflection of the way in which God wants to work in the world today.

Praise:

- ✧ I declare Jesus Christ as a man accredited by God by miracles, wonders and signs (Acts 2:22). I worship Jesus as the Son of God.
- ✧ Thank you Jesus for being willing to go to the cross and give up Your life for my redemption.
- ✧ I also declare Jesus Christ as risen from the dead. He has conquered death, disease, the Devil, and despair.

Thanksgiving:

- ✧ Jesus, I thank You that You didn't leave Your followers alone when You ascended into heaven. You gave them the gift of the Holy Spirit. I thank You that this promise of a helper/counselor is for me as well (Acts 2:38–39).
- ✧ God, I thank You for the promise that in the last days You will pour out Your Spirit on all flesh. I thank You that You can do miracles in my life through the person of the Holy Spirit today.
- ✧ I thank You for these miracles and answers to prayer that I have experienced in the past. (Name specific instances that come to mind.)

Confession:

✧ Just as the 120 people in the upper room prepared themselves for a great outpouring of the Holy Spirit, I ask You to reveal anything that might hinder Your work in my life. I turn from these and ask Your cleansing in my life:
- Disunity among brothers (bitterness, gossip)
- Self-gratification, sexual sin, lust
- Grumbling, doubt, ingratitude
- Hurt that I have caused and not made restitution for

✧ Lord, You promised that if I repented and turned to You, that times of refreshing would come. May it be so (Acts 3:19–20).

Requests:

✧ **Outpouring:** Just as You poured out Your Spirit in Acts 2, may You pour out Your Spirit on my life, on my home, and on my church.

✧ **Ingathering:** As a result, may there be a great harvest of souls. Pray for specific people who need Jesus Christ as their Savior.

✧ **Miracles:** May You also do signs and wonders today for those who have needs. Pray for those who need a healing or miracle of some type. Be specific.

✧ **Life:** Just as the early church in Jerusalem was living in community and enjoying an abundance of personal growth, may You fill my life with strong spiritual relationships, provide a greater revelation of Your Word, and increase my capacity in prayer. Bless my small group and my church with a fresh touch from heaven.

✧ **Relief:** One of the signs of the early church was generosity and care for the poor and hurting. Lord, reveal to me the person You might want me to help today. Pray for provision for those you know are in need.

✧ **Vision:** One of the promises of outpouring is visions and dreams for the future. May You open my eyes to the fullness of my destiny. May You fulfill the destiny of my family and open their eyes with fresh vision. May You surround me and those under my care with Your protective hedge against all attack.

✧ **Missions:** Just as You did on the day of Pentecost, may the message of Christ extend to the nations of the earth. Pray for specific nations and specific missionaries and their needs

Praise:

✧ I worship You, as the God of the harvest. Thank you, that You love me. Thank You that You love people. I praise You, in advance, for the powerful works You are going to do in my life today.

DAY 28

PRAYING PSALM 103

Background: Psalm 103 is one of the great biblical declarations of praise. On this day of worship, use these verses to declare God's goodness in your world.

Read Psalm 103 aloud.

Praise: *"Praise the Lord, my soul; all my inmost being, praise his holy name"* (v. 1). (Begin with a song.)

Thanksgiving: *"forget not all his benefits"* (vv. 2–5)

✧ Thank God for forgiveness, for health, and for His redeeming work in your life.

✧ Reflect on the good things that He is satisfying you with currently.

Prayer Focus:

✧ God, may You work righteousness and justice for the oppressed (v. 6). (Pray for a people group or individual who needs God's deliverance.)

✧ May You reveal to me Your ways like You revealed them to Moses. I want to know who You are (v. 7).

✧ May You reveal to Your people Your great deeds. (Pray for miracles in your life, your family, and your church.)

Declare God's Love and Grace:

✧ I thank You God that You are compassionate and gracious, slow to anger and abounding in love (v. 8).

✧ You do not always accuse nor do You harbor Your anger forever. You do not treat me as my sins deserve, nor repay me according to my iniquities (vv. 9–10).

- ✧ As high as the heavens are above the earth, so great is Your love for me because I fear You (v. 11).
- ✧ As far as the east is from the west, so far have You removed my transgressions from me (v. 12).
- ✧ As an earthly father has compassion on his children, so You have compassion on my life (v. 13).

Consider Life In View Of Eternity: (vv.14–16)

- ✧ What are you doing today that will count forever?
- ✧ How are you investing your time, talent, and treasure in the kingdom?

Prayer Focus: *"From everlasting to everlasting the Lord's love is with those who fear him"* (v. 17).

- ✧ Pray for those who need to experience the saving love of Jesus.
- ✧ Pray for your children and for future generations that they might be saved and experience the full benefits of covenant relationship with the Almighty (v. 18).
- ✧ Pray for your leaders, your pastors, and any government officials that they would learn to obey God's precepts.

Praying God's Rule: *"The Lord has established his throne in heaven, and his kingdom rules over all"* (v. 19).

- ✧ May Your kingdom come in me and Your will be done in my life as it is in heaven. I surrender to You.
- ✧ May You rule over my home, family, and all that is under my care.
- ✧ May You rule over my church and small group.
- ✧ May You rule over my community, workplace, and neighborhood.
- ✧ May You rule in this nation. May the glory of the Lord cover the earth as the waters cover the sea (Isaiah 11:9).

Praise: End with a song and some declarations (vv. 20–22).

- ✧ Praise the Lord, you His angels, you mighty ones who do His bidding, who obey His word.
- ✧ Praise the Lord all His heavenly hosts, you His servants who do His will.
- ✧ Praise the Lord, all His works, everywhere in His dominion.
- ✧ Praise the Lord, O my soul.

DAY 29

PRAYING PSALM 116

Background: Psalm 116 is packed with tremendous observations about how God operates within our lives. This psalm triggers strong thoughts of thanksgiving and clear pictures of how and what we should pray.

Praise: *"I love the Lord . . ."*

- ✧ *"for he heard my voice; he heard my cry for mercy"* (v. 1). Thank You God that You are always available to me. You are committed to my well-being.

- ✧ *"because He turned his ear to me, I will call on Him as long as I live"* (v. 2). Thank You, God, for giving me life. You are the sustainer of all that I have.

Thanksgiving: Thank God for all He has done in your life.

- ✧ **Salvation:** *"The cords of death entangled me, the anguish of the grave came over me"* (v. 3). When I was in great need, You saved me!

- ✧ **Comfort/Provision:** *"I was overcome by distress and sorrow. Then I called on the name of the Lord, 'Lord, save me'"* (vv. 3–4). (Recount your many answers to prayer.)

- ✧ **God's Trustworthy Character:** *"The Lord is gracious and righteous; our God is full of compassion"* (v. 5).

- ✧ **God's Constant Protection:** *"The Lord protects the unwary; when I was brought low, he saved me"* (v. 6). I choose to simply put my trust in You, Lord. Protect me and all my family today.

Meditation: *"Return to your rest, my soul, for the Lord has been good to you" (v. 7).* (Think on and list all of the many small or large daily signs of God's goodness in your life.)

Prayer for Victory/Deliverance: *"For you, Lord, have delivered me from death, my eyes from tears, my feet from stumbling, that I may walk before the Lord in the land of the living" (vv. 8–9).*

- ✧ I declare God's victory over areas of temptation in my life today. I set my heart today to obey God and to delight in His presence.
- ✧ I confess any sin in my life. I ask You, Lord, to cleanse my heart and mind.
- ✧ I pray God's hedge of protection against the attack of the Enemy in my life and in the lives of those under my care.

Prayer for Healing: *"I trusted in the Lord when I said, 'I am greatly afflicted'; in my alarm I said, 'Everyone is a liar'" (vv. 10–11).* But I know that God is ever true to His Word.

- ✧ Pray for specific people who need healing.
- ✧ Pray for specific people who need salvation. God is not willing that any should perish.
- ✧ Pray for those who are walking through trial.

Advanced Decision Making: *"What shall I return to the Lord for all His goodness to me? I will lift up the cup of salvation and call on the name of the Lord. I will fulfill my vows to the Lord in the presence of all his people" (vv. 12–14).*

- ✧ God, show me what I need to do to adjust the way I spend my time, my talents, and my finances.
- ✧ Show me if I am keeping a day of Sabbath and spending enough time with God.
- ✧ Help me be faithful to tithe and give to those in need.
- ✧ *"Precious in the sight of the Lord is the death of his faithful servants" (v. 15).* (Consider whether you are living your life in light of eternity today.)

✧ *"Truly I am Your servant, Lord; I serve you just as my mother did; you have freed me from my chains"* (v. 16). (Consider whether Jesus is truly your master.)

✧ Lord I am waiting on You for Your specific instructions. I choose to obey Your voice.

Thanksgiving/Praise:

✧ *"I will sacrifice a thank offering to you and call on the name of the Lord"* (v. 17). I choose to live this day in sacrificial worship. I will go above and beyond the call today.

✧ *"I will fulfill my vows to the Lord in the presence of all his people, in the courts of the house of the Lord—in your midst, Jerusalem* [the place where I dwell]*"* (vv. 18–19).

✧ I set my course to avoid things that grieve God's heart and live today to please the Father.

✧ *"Praise the Lord"* (v. 19). I choose to praise You, Lord, all throughout this day.

DAY 30

PRAYING PSALM 57

Background: Psalm 57 is a declaration of dependence on God. It recognizes that relationship with God means everything. If God is exalted in my life, then I will be lifted up in the process. So I worship my way through my trials and pain.

Worship: *"Have mercy on me, my God, have mercy on me, for in you I take refuge. I will take refuge in the shadow of your wings until the disaster has passed"* (v. 1).

- ✧ I praise You because You are a God of great mercy. You forgive my faults. You look past my failures.
- ✧ You are a refuge for my soul. Even when there are disastrous situations, You keep me safe in Your care.
- ✧ I choose to trust You to see me through the challenges of my world today.

Prayers of Agreement: *"I cry out to God Most High, to God, who vindicates me [fulfills His purpose for me]"* (v. 2).

- ✧ Fulfill Your purpose for my life O God. May Your Kingdom come in me and Your will be done in my life as it is in the heavens.
- ✧ May You bring to pass every good promise You have declared toward me and my family.
- ✧ Fulfill Your purpose for my loved ones (call them each by name). May You prosper (names) and cause them to be in health even as their soul prospers.

Prayers of Protection: *"He sends from heaven and saves me, rebuking those who hotly pursue me—God sends forth his love and his faithfulness. I am in the midst of lions; I am forced to dwell among ravenous beasts—men whose teeth are spears and arrows, whose tongues are sharp swords"* (vv. 3–4).

✧ God, may You send Your angels from heaven to protect me and all those under my care from any attack from the evil one.

✧ May Your faithfulness be like a shield around me and my family.

✧ You said in Isaiah 54:17 that no weapon formed against me will prevail, but that I will refute every tongue that accuses me and enjoy the full inheritance as a child of God.

Prayers for Exaltation/Victory: *"They spread a net for my feet—I was bowed down in distress. They dug a pit in my path—but they have fallen into it themselves. . . . Be exalted, O God, above the heavens; let Your glory be over all the earth"* (vv. 6 and 11)

✧ When I don't know what to pray for, I simply ask for my God to be exalted. So be exalted, O God, in my trials and difficulties.

✧ I tie my life to You O God. As You are exalted, I believe that I will rise and triumph with You.

✧ Be exalted above the heavens, and may Your glory be over and completely throughout my world. May Your glory fill my house, my neighborhood, and my workplace (or school).

✧ Draw my friends (list by name) to the saving knowledge of Jesus Christ.

Meditation on God's Goodness: Take time to think about God's goodness in your life and thank Him for it.

Prayers for Cleansing and Stability: *"My heart, O God, is steadfast, my heart is steadfast; I will sing and make music"* (v. 7).

✧ I choose to trust God and not to fear. I will not let fear rule my imaginations. I choose to believe God.

✧ I choose to run to God for relief and comfort and not to do anything sinful. God, forgive me for times when I have run from You to find relief.

✧ I choose to worship and not to complain. When tempted to despair, I will worship today. When I am tempted to worry, I will pray. I will be steadfast.

Worship: *"Awake, my soul! Awake, harp and lyre! I will awaken the dawn. I will praise you, Lord, among the nations; I will sing of you among the peoples. For great is your love, reaching to the heavens; your faithfulness reaches to the skies. Be exalted, O God, above the heavens; let your glory be over all the earth"* (vv. 8–11).

DAY 31

PRAYING UNSHAKABLE QUALITIES

Background: Peter, who was one of Jesus' disciples, wrote two letters to the churches. In the first few verses of his second letter, he provides a list of things that make us strong and unshakable. Today, we will pray for these qualities, which are God's will for us, to be released into our lives.

Read 2 Peter 1:2–9

Praise and Thanksgiving:

- ✧ God, I thank You for the abundance of grace and peace that I have in Jesus Christ. I choose to walk in that sufficient grace and fully receive Your prevailing peace.
- ✧ Thank You that through the power of the Holy Spirit, You have already given me all that I need for life.
- ✧ Thank You also for the precious promises of God that are like a solid rock foundation for me to live in victory over sin and evil, allowing me to experience the full and abundant life that You desire for me.

Focus #1: Pray for Faith

- ✧ I declare today my conviction that Jesus is the Son of God, who died for my sins on the cross, was buried, and raised on the third day.
- ✧ I declare not only that Jesus is alive, but that He has conquered sin, death, disease, and every enemy that stands against me.
- ✧ I choose to fill my life with God's Word, knowing that my faith grows by hearing and hearing comes by the Word of God (see Romans 10:17).

Focus #2: Pray for Virtue

✧ I confess any area of sin that the Holy Spirit reveals in my life. (Consider the various areas where you sin: words, actions, attitudes, thoughts.)

✧ God, I ask you to forgive me and to give me the strength of character to live above sin today.

✧ I choose to forgive those who have offended me. I release the hurt to you, O God, and ask you to heal any area of hurt and bitterness in me.

Focus #3: Pray for Intimacy with Christ (knowledge)

✧ Lord, I want to know You more than anything else. Grant me a greater awareness of your presence.

✧ Holy Spirit, speak into my life today. (Take a moment to listen to the prompting of the Holy Spirit. What is He saying to you today? Write down what He is speaking into your life.)

Focus #4: Pray for Unshakeable Qualities

✧ Lord, now build me into an unshakeable follower of Christ. Birth in me self-control, patience, godliness, kindness, and love.

✧ I ask You, God, to reveal to me ways in which I can demonstrate these qualities in my life today.

✧ Jesus, as I am connected to You (the Vine, John 15), cause my life to bear much fruit. Lord, glorify Your name in my life.

Focus #5: Pray for Specific Needs

✧ Pray for personal needs

✧ Pray for specific family needs

✧ Pray for people who need Jesus Christ as Savior

✧ Pray for financial breakthrough and blessing

✧ Pray for your small group and specific needs that people in the group have today

✧ Pray for your church and your pastors

✧ Pray for mission needs

PRAYING TO TEAR DOWN STRONGHOLDS

*"***F***or though we live in the world, we do not wage war as the world does. The weapons we fight with are not the weapons of the world. On the contrary, they have divine power to demolish strongholds. We demolish arguments and every pretension that sets itself up against the knowledge of God, and we take captive every thought to make it obedient to Christ"* (2 Corinthians 10:3–5).

I tear down the stronghold of **spiritual blindness**. Lift the veil that covers the eyes of people in this community and this city. Remove the blinders of guilt, shame, fear, and works-based religion. Shine the light of the glory of Jesus Christ so people would experience the grace that saves and the truth that sets them free. Lift the veil that covers the eyes of believers as well, and help them see the clear path of spiritual growth and blessing that is before them. Lift the blinders off unbelievers, and cause there to be a tremendous harvest of souls in every gospel-preaching church in the area. Draw people from the north, the south, the east, and the west. Bring them to the saving knowledge of Jesus Christ.

I tear down the stronghold of **unbelief**. Break the spirit of poverty that hangs in the atmosphere over our city. Reveal the truth that You have plans for us, to prosper us and not to harm us, to give us as individuals, our families, and our region a future and a hope. Burn into us Your promises. Give our city a fresh vision of the future and the courage to shake off the defeat of the past and reach toward the potential of the future. Bless us. Enlarge our territory in business, in finances, in spiritual life, in the church, and in our vision for future generations. Let Your hand be upon us. Deliver this city from evil and free us from the identity of past pain. We will not be limited by the failures, the challenges, or the defeated mentality of the past. We will rise to be all that God has for us.

I tear down the stronghold of **depression**. The joy of the Lord will be our strength. I shake off the spirit of heaviness and put on the garment of praise. I shake off the atmosphere of depression that hovers over this region. I declare a breakthrough in the heavenly realms. My life will be marked with praise and with joy. My home will be marked by an atmosphere of life and of hope. My neighborhood will have an open heaven over it and a tangible sense of God's presence in it. My church will be a place of celebration, favor, and life. This city will be filled with the glory of the Lord as the waters cover the sea.

PRAYING PSALM 51

PRAYERS FOR REPENTANCE

Background: David prayed these words after his great failure with Bathsheba. This psalm is all about redemption, forgiveness, and restoration.

Praise: *"Have mercy on me, O God . . ."* (v. 1)

- ✧ *"according to Your unfailing love . . ."* (v. 1). I praise You because You are a God who chooses to love me no matter what. You love me by choice and not because of my performance (good or bad).
- ✧ *"according to your great compassion blot out my transgressions"* (v. 1). God I praise You because You are passionate about me. You care deeply about my well-being.
- ✧ You are almighty, holy, and just! And yet, You are mercy, and love, and compassion.

Confession: *"Blot out my transgressions. Wash away all my iniquity and cleanse me from my sin"* (vv. 1–2).

- ✧ Transgression is defined as willful disobedience to God's law. I repent of any willful sin in my life. (Be specific.)
- ✧ Iniquity is going my own way, doing my own thing. I repent of a self-centered heart. I surrender to God's leadership in every area of my life.
- ✧ Sin is any area where I miss the mark. I confess to God any attitudes, words, or actions that need to be put under the blood of Jesus.

Thanksgiving: *"For I know my transgressions and my sin is always before me"* (v. 3). (Yet You have forgiven me time and again.)

✧ *"Against you, you only have I sinned and done what is evil in your sight"* (v. 4). Yet You continue to pursue me. Thank you, God, for not giving up on me.

✧ *"So you are right in your verdict and justified when you judge"* (v. 4). I thank You that You are pure, holy, without evil intent, a God of integrity.

✧ *"Surely I was sinful at birth, sinful from the time my mother conceived me"* (v. 5). Yet You died for me anyway. I am so unworthy, but You gave Your all to save me.

✧ *"Yet you desired faithfulness even in the womb; you taught me wisdom in that secret place"* (v. 6). I thank You that You are committed to repairing/sanctifying my soul.

Declaration of Forgiveness:

✧ *"Cleanse me with hyssop and I will be clean"* (v. 7). (Hyssop is a very common plant which speaks of faith—because God has given everyone a measure of faith.)

✧ I realize I cannot earn forgiveness but I receive it by faith in Jesus.

✧ *"Wash me, and I will be whiter than snow"* (v. 7). I choose to declare myself as clean by the blood of Jesus. No guilt or stain remains on me.

✧ *"Hide your face from my sins and blot out my iniquity"* (v. 9). I choose to do the same. I forgive myself and choose to move on with my life.

Request for Restoration:

✧ *"Create in me a pure heart, O God, and renew a steadfast spirit within me"* (v. 10). Give me the right desires. Cause me to want the right things.

✧ *"Do not cast me from your presence or take your Holy Spirit from me"* (v. 11). Fill my life, O God. I need you.

✧ *"Restore to me the joy of your salvation"* (v. 12). I choose joy today and not dread. I will live in anticipation of your goodness.

✧ *"Grant me a willing spirit to sustain me"* (v. 12).

Prayer Focus: *"Then I will teach transgressors your ways, so that sinners will turn back to you"* (v. 13).

✧ Pray for salvation for those who need Christ. (Be specific.)

✧ Pray for those who have fallen away to return. (Be specific.)

✧ Pray for your family that God would draw them to Himself.

Praise: Read Psalm 51:14–19.

✧ Thank You Jesus that your sacrifice on the cross is enough. Your blood that was shed for me saves me.

✧ Thank You that You do not want a sacrifice from me. I cannot earn Your love. You simply want my contrite heart.

✧ I praise you because you are committed to your people (me, my family, my church) even when we fail you.

LIFE TRANSFORMATION PRAYER

ord of Glory, I want to be transformed by Your Presence in my life. Wash over my mind with the promises of Your Word. Renew me by Your Holy Spirit. My desire is for our friendship to grow stronger and stronger each day.

Jesus, be my best friend. I want Your love to be the fire that burns within me. Possess my soul and consume me more and more. Breathe within my heart the life that only You can give. I long to know You in a greater way—reveal Yourself to me. In Jesus' name, Amen.

DECLARATIONS:

✧ God is going to lead me into a major season of spiritual breakthrough. I will experience miracles of healing, salvation, restoration, and deliverance. Lives, marriages, and families will be touched for Christ.

✧ May Your kingdom (all of heaven's resources) come and Your will (the fullness of Your promise and purpose) be done in my life, my family, my church, and this region, in Jesus name. May heaven be released on our behalf.

✧ I declare that *suddenly* the power of God will be released, people will be healed, miracles will occur as signs that point to Jesus, and that many of my family and friends will be saved. I declare this in the name of Jesus Christ!

✧ Lord, I declare that You will be publicly endorsed in my city, in my community, and among my family and friends by doing wonderful miracles and signs.

✧ Lord, I declare that You will fulfill Acts 2:17–18 in my

life. Pour out Your Spirit on me. Cause me to dream God-sized dreams and to be filled with Spirit-inspired vision.

✧ I am not alone. God will carry me all the way through until the end.

✧ I have great authority. God sends me into life with His complete backing and total support.

✧ I am not defined by my past, my present, or my natural limitations: God defines me as a mighty warrior! And I agree with Him!

FAMILY PRAYER

- ✧ God, I am declaring Your power and promise over my future generations.
- ✧ Bring life where there is struggle, freedom where there is bondage, wisdom and revelation where there is confusion, and strength of character where there is weakness.
- ✧ You are a God who is able to forgive, redeem, and restore.
- ✧ May You do what only You can do in my family.
- ✧ Rebuke every attack against us.
- ✧ Fulfill every promise You have made concerning us.

In Jesus' name, amen!

ENDNOTES

1. Bruce Wilkinson, *The Prayer of Jabez: Breaking Through to the Blessed Life* (Colorado Springs, CO: Multnomah, 2000), 11.

2. Bill Hybels, *Who You Are When No One's Looking: Choosing Consistency, Resisting Compromise* (Downers Grove, IL: IVP, 2010), 31.

3. Wayne Cordiero, *The Divine Mentor: Growing Your Faith as You Sit at the Feet of the Savior* (Bloomington, MN: Bethany House Publishers, 2008).

4. If you are interested, you can buy a journal with the S.O.A.P. pattern built right into the pages.

5. The concepts in this day of prayer were adapted from, Rick Warren, *The Purpose Driven Life* (Grand Rapids, MI: Zondervan, 2002).

ABOUT THE AUTHOR

For the past twenty-four years, Jeff Leake has served as the lead pastor of Allison Park Church, which is a multicampus church in the city of Pittsburgh, PA. What is most notable about Jeff's ministry is his role in starting new churches and ministry organizations. Fifty new churches have been planted in the last twenty years out of the church planting movement initiated at Allison Park Church.

In 2011, Jeff founded Reach Northeast with a goal of planting 100 new churches in the Northeastern USA within a ten-year period of time. He established several other organizations to support this church planting movement: The Network of Hope is a nonprofit committed to seeing lasting change come to individuals, communities, and families in need; The Northeast Ministry School is a nine-month school devoted to developing church planters, church planting teams, ministers, and missionaries.

Jeff Leake holds an MA in missiology from the Assemblies of God Theological Seminary. He is the author of three books: *God In Motion*, *The Question That Changed My Life*, and *Learning to Follow Jesus*. He and his wife, Melodie, reside in Allison Park, PA.

Record of Prayer Requests and Answers to Prayer

Date: Request: Date: Answered Prayer:

Date: Request: Date: Answered Prayer:

Date: Request: Date: Answered Prayer:

Date: Request: Date: Answered Prayer:

Date: Request: Date: Answered Prayer:

Date: Request: Date: Answered Prayer:

Date: Request: Date: Answered Prayer:

FOR MORE INFORMATION

For more information about these and other valuable resources visit www.salubris-resources.com

In *God in Motion*, Jeff reminds us that even when God seems inactive, unaware, or indifferent, He is not. He is always in motion behind the scenes to accomplish His wonderful (if sometimes mysterious) purposes.

God in Motion contains inspiring life principles, compelling stories, specific applications, and questions to stimulate reflection and interaction. If you're puzzled about the loose ends in life . . . this book is for you!